Romans 8:14-16
Ruth Pettengill James

WHO AM I?

What is man that You take thought of him,
And the son of man that You care for him?
Yet You have made him a little lower than God,
And You crown him with glory and majesty!
You make him to rule over the works of Your hands;
You have put all things under his feet.

Psalm 8:4–6 (NASB)

RUTH PETTENGILL JAMES

Who Am I?

Trilogy Christian Publishers A Wholly Owned Subsidiary of Trinity Broadcasting Network

2442 Michelle Drive Tustin, CA 92780

DEDICATION

I dedicate this book to my mom, Mabel Elizabeth Gardner Pettengill (1915–2003). My mom demonstrated the love of Christ through her actions and words. In addition, my mom displayed the character of Mary and Martha of Bethany as she served others. She was the Proverbs 31 woman. She and I traveled together, experiencing spiritual retreats and journeys that I treasure. Near the end of her life, she told me that I was "the bravest woman she had ever known." Until we meet again—Mom, I love and miss you!

She is clothed with strength and dignity,
and she laughs without fear of the future.
When she speaks, her words are wise,
and she gives instructions with kindness.
She carefully watches everything in her household
and suffers nothing from laziness.
Her children stand and bless her.
Her husband praises her:
"There are many virtuous and capable women in
the world,
but you surpass them all!"
Charm is deceptive, and beauty does not last;
but a woman who fears the Lord will be greatly
praised.
Proverbs 31:25–30 (NLT)

ACKNOWLEDGMENTS

On the last Sunday of September 2021, during praise and worship at my church, I heard the Spirit of the Lord whisper to me, "Publish *Who Am I?*" My immediate thought was, *All right*, even though I knew I did not have the knowledge or the money to do it. After church, someone handed me a small, sealed envelope as I left the church. I thanked them, and when I arrived home, I opened the envelope to find a check that was almost large enough to publish the book. The check was from someone I had never met. At once, I knew that Jesus was in control of publishing the book. So my first thank you goes to Jesus Christ, my Savior and Lord, for trusting me with this book project. He has led me and given me the knowledge, people, and resources to complete this project.

As I wander through this process, I want to thank a few special people who encouraged and helped me. Anna K., Eric and Cerissa S., Michael H., Jackie C., and Archie M. helped me more than they knew. And I could not have even begun this project without my readers and their input. Thank you, Barbara K., Suzanne L., Sharon E., and Dale B. Your input has been invaluable. Nancy M., thank you for the little brown teapot that has sustained me while I learned to write a book and complete the process. And finally, for all the others too numerous to mention by name, I thank you all! God uses many people to accomplish His plans and purposes; for that, I am grateful.

TABLE OF CONTENTS

Preface. 9

Chapter 1: Introduction. 13

Chapter 2: Who Is God? 23

Chapter 3: Who Is God—Our Father? 37

Chapter 4: Who Is Jesus Christ? 45

Chapter 5: Who Is the Holy Spirit? 59

Chapter 6: What Are God's Characteristics? 73

Chapter 7: What Characteristics Did God Give Me? 91

Chapter 8: How Did God Make Me? 113

Chapter 9: What Are God's Gifts to Me? 139

Chapter 10: Why Is My Life Such a Mess? 147

Chapter 11: Is There Any Hope for Me? 159

Chapter 12: What Is God's Plan of Redemption? 167

Chapter 13: Why Is Water Baptism Important? 179

Chapter 14: What Is the Baptism of the Holy Spirit? . . . 189

Chapter 15: What Does It Mean to Be in Christ? 205

Chapter 16: What Is My Purpose? 221

Chapter 17: This Is Who I Am! 231

Bibliography 233

About the Author. 235

Scripture Index 237

PREFACE

In thinking about *Who Am I?* I began asking myself why I wrote this book in the first place. Some years ago, I was concerned about the number of people who had no idea who they were. Young girls and women were trying to look and act like supermodels, dieting to be slim and trim, whether that was their body style or not. They wanted to look and act like the rich and famous. Young boys and men tried to follow in the footsteps of their favorite public figures—handsome and wealthy. Peer pressure was and still is rampant in society and can be very destructive. If you do not look and act like others, you are marginalized, criticized, or made to feel worthless. God created you to be one of a kind for His plans for your life.

You can be the most beautiful, handsome, and talented person in the world, but that does not make you happy or successful. And it certainly doesn't make you feel loved or lovable. When you try to be someone other than who God made you be, you set yourself up for failure, depression, and feelings that you are not good enough. Today, many people suffer from various levels of low self-esteem. They feel worthless, like a failure, with no options for change because they do not know who God made them.

Some years ago, after the murder of my father and a painful divorce, I was unable to emotionally handle the loss and grief, causing everything in my life to be out of control. Thinking I had no options to change things, I attempted suicide. Instead of death, I went into heaven, where I stood before Jesus. I experienced the overwhelming, boundless love He had for me as I stood there. Later, as I considered this heavenly experience, I concluded that trying to be perfect in every area of my life, spending years in therapy, or chasing after worldly success and the feel-good lifestyle was not making me happy. I concluded that only God had the answers to my happiness. Some people will tell you that you are responsible for your happiness, and that is partially true, but only when you recognize and accept that God made you perfect in every way can you be happy.

You may have lived that perfect life, or you may not have experienced any tragedy like I did, but you know someone who has. Someone who is fearful, hurting, or has low self-esteem. People are searching for who they are and how to feel worthy and lovable. I pray that each person who reads this book will discover who they are and how wonderful they are. They will know how to obtain true happiness and peace, then share it with others. I know who I am in Christ. Now it is time for you, dear reader, to discover who you are in Christ.

For You formed my inward parts;
You wove me in my mother's womb.
I will give thanks to You, for I am fearfully and
wonderfully made;
Wonderful are Your works,
And my soul knows it very well.
My frame was not hidden from You,
When I was made in secret,

And skillfully wrought in the depths of the earth;
Your eyes have seen my unformed substance;
And in Your book were all written
The days that were ordained for me,
When as yet there was not one of them.
How precious also are Your thoughts to me, O God!
How vast is the sum of them!
If I should count them, they would outnumber the
sand.
When I awake, I am still with You.
Psalm 139:13–18 (NASB)

Galatians 3:28 (NIV), "There is neither Jew nor
Gentile, neither slave nor free, nor is there male and
female, for you are all one in Christ Jesus."

CHAPTER 1:

INTRODUCTION

Have you ever asked the question, "Who am I?" I have because I ask questions and always have. I am a curious person. As a child, when the family would travel, I would ask my dad questions like, "Are we there yet?" or "How much farther do we have to go?" One day, my Dad gave me a roadmap marked with our starting and ending points. He said, "Watch the road signs and follow the map, then you will know when we arrive." Needless to say, I can read a roadmap.

God gives us a roadmap for what our life can be and where we can go, but many of us have no idea who God is or who He says we are. We only know what others tell us—whether true or not. We look at the world and cultures around us and wonder why our life is too busy, too messy, too angry, or whatever emotion passes through us at that moment. We often have the mindset of, "Whatever will be, will be!" But God wants more for us. Without knowing where we began and where we will finish, we cannot know who or where we are on the road of life. Thankfully, God's Word tells us exactly who we are, where we are going, and how to get there.

As a Christian minister and missionary, I have found that people are the same around the world. Fathers and mothers love each other and their children. They work hard to provide for and protect their families. Children go to school, play, and sometimes even work in the family business. Yet children grow up and begin traveling on life's road without knowing who they truly are or where they are going. Today, many people have no actual knowledge of who God is. Therefore, without even thinking about it, people of all nations and cultures ask, "Who am I?" "Who is God?" "Why is my life such a mess?" "What is my purpose for being here?" "Where am I going, and where will I end up?"

Dear reader, as *you* read this book, I believe you will find the answers to these questions, and you will learn who you are and who our great God is. You will travel from the beginning of the book of Genesis to the end of Revelation to discover how God made you and how He sees you. You will find out how and why some of the events of the Bible, both in the Old and the New Testament, affect you today and in your future. I believe that you will have a greater understanding of who God is, how much He loves you, and how wonderful He made you. In short, you will find out who you are.

I also pray that you see yourself as the beautiful

and unique person God intended you to be. He wants a personal relationship with you, just as Adam and Eve had in the garden of Eden. God also wants to spend time with you each day in the garden of your life. He wants you to understand that He has a purpose for your life. I also pray that you see the many blessings God has given you. Knowing these great truths will also make you aware of why your life is a mess.

Again, as you read this book, I urge you to read for comprehension, not speed. Ask the question, "God, what can I learn about You and me?" He wants you to know who He is and who you are. God uses ordinary people like you throughout the Bible. When you understand these principles in the Bible, your life will change. Then, you will honestly know how God made you. Consider this: *Suppose you are a believer of many years, a new believer, or even someone who knows nothing about Jesus. If so, you may think this is too much information, but if you continue reading to the end of this book, you will have answers to many of your questions.* All will become clear as you begin to understand your relationship with God and how important you are to Him.

With that said, if you are going to learn who you are, you need to go to the source, which is the Holy Bible—God's Word, also known as the Scriptures. *We will use a lot of scriptures in different translations to understand what God has to say to you and about you.* We will also define words that are important for your understanding. I will be using the online Merriam-Webster Dictionary for most of the definitions. In addition, I will use *you* and *yours* because this book is written primarily to you. Remember the Bible is essential for discovering the truth about God, who you are, and why His Word is important to you.

Second Timothy 3:16–17 (NKJV), "All Scripture is given by inspiration of God and is profitable for doctrine, for reproof, for correction, for instruction in righteousness, that the man of God may be complete, thoroughly equipped for every good work."

Before we go forward, you need to know there are hidden messages in the Bible that will be revealed to you so that you might learn more about who God is and who you are. He wants you to know His Word, thoughts, and will for you.

Amos 3:7 (NKJV), "Surely the Lord God does nothing Unless He reveals His secret to His servants the prophets."

When you listen to God's Word, He will tell you what you need to know. Listening to Him is like a small voice or thought inside you. For instance, have you ever started to leave your home in the morning with the sun shining brightly, and this thought comes to you, *Take your umbrella!* But you think it doesn't look like rain, so you do not take your umbrella. Then sometime later, it begins to rain; you wish you had listened to that small voice – the voice of God protecting you from being caught unaware. Some people call it your conscience, but it is the Spirit of God who gives you information on what is to come.

Many people have heard that old saying, "God works in mysterious ways, and it's not for us to know." But that is not true according to the Scriptures. Read these scriptures carefully to understand that God is not keeping you in the dark. He wants you to know what is happening.

Matthew 10:26 (NLT), "But don't be afraid of those who threaten you. For the time is coming when everything that is covered will be revealed, and all that is secret will be made known to all."

Mark 4:22–23 (NIV), "For whatever is hidden is meant to be disclosed, and whatever is concealed is meant to be brought out into the open. If anyone has ears to hear, let them hear."

Listen to what the apostle Paul had to say about things hidden:

And so it was with me, brothers and sisters. When I came to you, I did not come with eloquence or human wisdom as I proclaimed to you the testimony about God. For I resolved to know nothing while I was with you except Jesus Christ and him crucified. I came to you in weakness with great fear and trembling. My message and my preaching were not with wise and persuasive words, but with a demonstration of the Spirit's power, so that your faith might not rest on human wisdom, but on God's power. We do, however, speak a message of wisdom among the mature, but not the wisdom of this age or of the rulers of this age, who are coming to nothing. No, we declare God's wisdom, a mystery that has been hidden and that God destined for our glory before time began. None of the rulers of this age understood it, for if they had, they would not have crucified the Lord of glory.

1 Corinthians 2:1–8 (NIV)

Paul continued to tell the church at Corinth how God reveals His thoughts and ways to us by His Spirit: the Holy Spirit of God.

However, as it is written:

"What no eye has seen, what no ear has heard, and what no human mind has conceived"—

the things God has prepared for those who love him— these are the things God has revealed to us by his Spirit.

The Spirit searches all things, even the deep things of God. For who knows a person's thoughts except their own spirit within them? In the same way no one knows the thoughts of God except the Spirit of God. What we have received is not the spirit of the world, but the Spirit who is from God, so that we may understand what God has freely given us.

1 Corinthians 2:9–12 (NIV)

Paul told the people not to listen to the world's wisdom but to listen to God's Word as He reveals what we need to know about Him. The world's wisdom will fail you, but God's wisdom never fails.

Let us begin so you will learn how wonderfully and

uniquely God made you. *There is no one else on the planet just like you!* Even identical twins have differences. I have twin friends who look so much alike that when people see them separately in a group setting, they wonder if they might be seeing things. However, once you know them, you know the tiny differences in their looks and character. He designed you to be you so that you could reach your potential and your God-given destiny.

In the Old Testament, we meet a young woman named Esther, whom God called for a specific time and purpose. God has called you for such a time as this too! So let us look at Esther and her family to see how you might be like her. You can find her story in the Old Testament book of Esther, chapters 1–10.

The family of Esther was a typical Jewish family from the Tribe of Benjamin. This family was among the exiles taken into captivity when the Persians captured their lands, taking them to Babylon. History tells us that Esther, whose Jewish name was Hadassah, was about fourteen years old when she and her family were exiled to Babylon. In Babylon, she was given the Persian name of Esther, which means "a star." After her parents died, Esther became the ward of Mordecai, who was her uncle (Esther 2:7). He was an official of the Persian palace who raised her as his daughter. However, to protect her, Mordecai made her promise not to reveal that she was Jewish because some of the Persians hated the Jewish exiles.

The former queen of Persia, Vashti, disobeyed the king, who divorced her, then began a search for another queen.

Because of her great beauty, Esther was among the young women chosen to be considered the next queen of Persia. After a year of training and grooming, she was chosen and became the queen of King Ahasuerus (Xerxes I), who reigned from 486 to 465 BC. Sometime later, Mordecai uncovered a plot to kill the king but was removed from the palace before he could report it to the king. Haman, an evil palace official, lied about Mordecai, causing him to be removed from his position at the palace.

Haman not only wanted to kill the king, but He wanted to kill all the Jews in the kingdom too. When Mordecai heard this, he went to Esther in secret and told her to tell the king. However, to approach the king without his invitation meant death. Therefore, when Esther agreed to go to the king, she asked Mordecai to have the many Jews in the kingdom fast and pray with her for several days before approaching the king.

After prayer and fasting, Esther went to the king and found favor as she revealed Haman's plot. The king had Haman hung on the gallows Haman had constructed to hang Mordecai. Mordecai was restored to his official position, and the many Jews in the land found favor in the king's eyes.

The name of God never appears in the story of Esther, but it shows us that God's power, provision, and purposes will come to pass even when we cannot see Him working. Just as Esther was a star in her day, God has a plan for you to be "a star" in your day.

God also calls us the apple of His eye. As each person

protects and cares for their eyes, God protects and cares for you.

Psalm 17:8 (NKJV), "Keep me as the apple of Your eye; Hide me under the shadow of Your wings."

CHAPTER 2:

WHO IS GOD?

To understand who you are, you first need to know who God is. God is a supernatural spirit being that cannot be seen naturally. God is just as real as you or any other person, except higher laws instead of physical laws govern Him. *Spirit* means "breath"; God is the breath of life. Listen to what Jesus told the woman at a well in Samaria.

John 4:24 (NASB), "God is spirit, and those who worship Him must worship in spirit and truth."

Throughout the Bible, God is referred to with masculine pronouns such as *He* and *Him*, although like any other person, God has a name. There are many words that describe who He is and what He is like, but He is one God in three persons. Therefore, we will look at God as the one God with a three-part or triune nature. We will look at the three distinct personalities of God: God the Father, Jesus Christ the Son of God, and the Holy Spirit of God. The Father is not the Son or the Holy Spirit. The Son is not the Father or the Holy Spirit. The Holy Spirit is not the Father or the Son. Even though these persons can be identified separately, they function together as one God. It might sound confusing to you, but when we finish this chapter, I think you will have a good understanding of who our one God is. I also pray that you will know God the Father, Jesus the Son, and the Holy Spirit when you finish this book, just as well as you know yourself.

Let us begin the quest to know God by starting in the first book of the Holy Bible, the book of Genesis, with the family of Isaac's son Jacob. Jacob's estranged son Joseph was living in Egypt as a top official in the Egyptian government when a severe famine occurred in the land of Israel (Genesis 41–47). Knowing about the famine, Joseph invited his family to live in Egypt, where grain was abundant. So Jacob's family, consisting of seventy people, traveled to Egypt, where they lived in comfort for many years. God had previously changed Jacob's name to Israel (Genesis 32:28).

Four hundred and thirty years later, we find Jacob's descendants, called the children of Israel, as servants in severe bondage to a new Pharaoh, also known as the king of Egypt. They were crying out to God for mercy. So God selected a man named Moses to deliver the people out of Egypt.

> *And God said to Moses, "I AM WHO I AM."*
> *And He said, "Thus you shall say to the children of Israel, 'I AM has sent me to you.'"*
> *Moreover God said to Moses, "Thus you shall*

24

say to the children of Israel: 'The Lord God of your fathers, the God of Abraham, the God of Isaac, and the God of Jacob, has sent me to you. This is My name forever, my memorial to all generations.'"

Exodus 3:14–15 (NKJV)

When God called Moses to lead the children of Israel out of Egypt, God identified Himself as "I AM WHO I AM." What a strange way to identify yourself! However, these words told Moses that God's name declared that He was the eternal, living God with no beginning and no end, the everlasting God. These words speak of the timeless existence of God. He always was—and will be forever. He had no beginning, and He has no end. In addition, when God called Moses, He told Moses that He would be with him and help him. We see a reference to His timelessness again in the last book of the Holy Bible called the book of Revelation.

Revelation 1:4 (NKJV), "Grace to you and peace from Him who is and who was and who is to come…"

At the time of the Exodus, four hundred and thirty years after they moved to Egypt, the children of Israel had grown from seventy people to over six hundred thousand men plus their wives and children.

The Israelites journeyed from Rameses to Sukkoth. There were about six hundred thousand men on foot, besides women and children. Many other people went up with them with large droves of livestock, both flocks and herds. Now, the Israelite people had lived in Egypt for 430 years. At the end of the 430 years, to the very day, all the Lord's divisions left Egypt.

Exodus 12:37–38, 40–41 (NIV)

As you learn about God, it is essential to understand there is a *God-side* and a *man-side* to every action, promise, blessing, and curse. The God-side is God's responsibility, while the man-side is your responsibility.

Let us look first at the God-side of things. First, God is a covenant-making God. The online Merriman-Webster Dictionary defines a *covenant* as "a formal, binding agreement or promise between two or more parties for the performance of some action."

Now, let us go back to the book of Genesis, chapter 12, to meet Abram, later known as Abraham, to understand the Abrahamic Covenant.

The Lord had said to Abram, "Go from your country, your people, and your father's household to the land I will show you.

"I will make you into a great nation,

and I will bless you;

I will make your name great,

And you will be a blessing.

I will bless those who bless you,

and whoever curses you I will curse;

and all peoples on earth

will be blessed through you."

*So Abram went, as the Lord had told him, and
Lot went with him. Abram was seventy-five
years old when he set out from Harran.*

Genesis 12:1–4 (NIV)

About 2000 BC, Abram was seventy-five years old and
childless, living with his wife Sarai in Ur of the Chaldees,
a city located in southern Iraq, when God called him to
leave everything he had known.

*Abram fell facedown, and God said to him,
"As for me, this is my covenant with you: You
will be the father of many nations. No longer
will you be called Abram; your name will be
Abraham, for I have made you a father of
many nations. I will make you exceedingly
fruitful; I will make nations of you, and kings
will come from you.*

Genesis 17:3–6 (NIV)

God made a covenant of promise with Abram. This
covenant, called the Abrahamic Covenant, promised
Abraham that God would bless him and make him a great
nation. In addition, the covenant gave God a permanent
connection to man. Remember Abram was childless
when God created the covenant with him. The lesson
for you is that God can and sometimes does change your
circumstances. However, when and how God chooses to
make those changes is His choice. His desire is for you to
know and embrace His plans and purposes for your life.

As part of the covenant with Abram, God changed
Abram's name to Abraham, meaning the "Father of many

nations," which can also mean the "Father of a multitude" (Genesis 17:5, NKJV). This name change promised that the childless Abraham would have many children. In addition, the promise included that kings would come from his line; specifically, King David and Jesus would come from Abraham's line.

Matthew 1:1 (NIV), "This is the genealogy of Jesus the Messiah, the son of David, the son of Abraham."

This scripture tells us immediately that Jesus was a descendant of King David and Abraham. Let us follow some scriptures to see how this changed Abraham and, ultimately, you and me. This covenant of promise will last for a thousand generations—even to an everlasting covenant.

He remembers his covenant forever,

the promise he made, for a thousand generations,

the covenant he made with Abraham,

The oath he swore to Isaac.

He confirmed it to Jacob as a decree,

to Israel as an everlasting covenant:

Psalm 105:8–10 (NIV)

James 2:23 (NIV), "And the scripture was fulfilled that says, 'Abraham believed God, and it was credited to him as righteousness,' and he was called God's friend."

Not only was Abraham considered righteous by God, but Abraham was also called a *friend of God*. "How would you like to be called a *friend of God*?" Look at what the prophet Jeremiah said about the partners of the covenant.

> *They will be my people, and I will be their God. And I will give them one heart and one purpose: to worship me forever, for their own good and for the good of all their descendants. And I will make an everlasting covenant with them: I will never stop doing good for them. I will put a desire in their hearts to worship me, and they will never leave me. I will find joy doing good for them and will faithfully and wholeheartedly replant them in this land.*
>
> **Jeremiah 32:38–41 (NLT)**

But there is still more; the covenant promises God made with Abraham have not passed away. Many years later, Jesus, God's Son, fulfilled that covenant and ratified a new and better covenant for those who are called God's children.

Hebrews 10:16–17 (NKJV), "'This is the covenant that I will make with them after those days, says the Lord: I will put My laws into their hearts, and in their minds, I will write them,' then He adds, 'Their sins and their lawless deeds I will remember no more.'"

The Scriptures tell us that the new covenant is for the *Seed* of Abraham.

Galatians 3:16 (NKJV), "Now to Abraham and his Seed were the promises made. He does not say, 'And to seeds,' as of many, but as of one, 'And to your Seed,' who is Christ."

Galatians 3:29 (NKJV), "And if you are Christ's, then you are Abraham's seed, and heirs according to the promise."

When you are a believer in Jesus Christ as your Lord and Savior, you are part of the covenant of Abraham, and you and all other believers are called heirs to the promises God gave to Abraham. In a covenant relationship, the resources and strengths of the stronger party are for the benefit of the weaker party. For example, a king usually has more resources or strengths than his subjects. This concept made no sense until I traveled to an actual kingdom where I could see and understand how a kingdom works. In the United States of America, we live in a country ruled by the people, but the king has the ultimate authority to dictate how his people live in a kingdom. For instance, in the kingdom I visited, the king would not allow televisions in the people's homes because he did not want other cultures to influence his people. They were required to live under his rule and protection. Their lives were not bad, only different from ours because their freedom of choice was limited.

Let us go back to our study of God's covenant. If you are a believer, you are part of the Abrahamic Covenant. Jesus fulfilled that covenant and showed us a new and better covenant based on the promises of the Abrahamic Covenant. He wants to establish His new covenant with you, using His strength and provisions in place of your weakness and needs. To make sure you understand the covenant relationship with God, I want to define several words. These exact definitions might not be found in a dictionary but can be understood by studying God's Word.

The words *binding agreement* can mean "an obligation to perform an agreed course of action." Under a covenant, all parties must agree to the covenant conditions. A covenant is similar to a marriage contract where the husband and wife agree to forsake others. A covenant is like a contract to purchase a piece of property such as a house or a car. One party grants the property, while the other pays the agreed-upon price.

The online Merriam-Webster Dictionary explains that in a *promise*, "there is every reason to expect that something will happen in the future, such as an indication of future success or improvement."

Therefore, a promise is an agreement, written or spoken, by someone who will do what they say they will do. In some circles, it is a handshake agreement because it is their bond or pledge to do whatever they have said they would do. But like a binding agreement, it can also mean "a legally binding declaration that gives the person the right to expect or claim a specific act's performance."

The online Merriam-Webster Dictionary also defines *action* as an act of will, "a thing done; the accomplishment of a thing usually over time, or in stages, or with the possibility of repetition." Regardless of how long it takes, we act on whatever we deem important, such as completing a project or finishing a creative project.

The online Merriam-Webster Dictionary defines

blessing as "a thing conducive to happiness or welfare." A blessing allows or helps you to do something or to be successful, something that brings you happiness, approval, or encouragement. Blessings make things you do seem easy rather than complex.

Again, the online Merriam-Webster Dictionary defines *curse* as "to bring harm, injury, or misfortune to another." It means you are hindered or unsuccessful at every turn. It is also important to know that sometimes we are unsuccessful in what we attempt, not because of a curse, but because it is not the right thing to do or the right timing. There are other kinds of curses, but we are only talking about Biblical curses in this book.

Let us look into the Holy Bible to find out more about our three-in-one God.

Genesis 1:1 (NKJV), "In the beginning God created the heavens and the earth."

Psalm 24:1 (NKJV), "The earth is the Lord's, and all its fullness, The world and those who dwell therein."

Romans 11:36 (NLT), "For everything comes from him and exists by his power and is intended for his glory. All glory to him forever! Amen."

In the Old Testament's original language of Hebrew, the word *God* in Genesis 1:1 is *Eloheim*—the first covenant name of God. *Eloheim* has both singular and plural meanings. The plural sense refers to rulers or judges with divine connections. Used here, it is the particular name of God but with a plural meaning referring to God the

Father, Jesus Christ, the Son of God, also known as the *Word*, and the Holy Spirit (Zodhiates 1984, 1578).

First John 5:7–8 (NKJV), "For there are three that bear witness in heaven: the Father, the Word, and the Holy Spirit; and these three are one. And there are three that bear witness on earth: the Spirit, the water, and the blood; and these three agree as one."

In this scripture, the *Word* refers to Jesus Christ as explained in John, chapter 1. Therefore, there is only one eternal God in three persons who created the earth, man, and everything in existence. *Eloheim* is one of His various names that reveal His character.

> *In the beginning was the Word, and the Word was with God, and the Word was God. He was in the beginning with God. All things came into being through Him, and apart from Him nothing came into being that has come into being. In Him was life, and the life was the Light of men. The Light shines in the darkness, and the darkness did not comprehend it. And the Word became flesh, and dwelt among us, and we saw His glory, glory as of the only begotten from the Father, full of grace and truth.*
>
> **John 1:1–5, 14 (NASB)**

These three supernatural persons are equal in all their attributes, such as holiness, love, truth, justice, and much more. They are infinite, boundless, and eternal. They are in unity and harmony with each other but with separate functions. They all were equally active in the work of creation and redemption. But there is more: God created you in His image. So you have three parts: you have a spirit, which is your inner man or woman; you have a soul consisting of your mind, your free will, and your emotions; and you live in a physical body.

Ephesians 4:4–6 (NIV), "There is one body and one Spirit, just as you were called to one hope when you were called; one Lord, one faith, one baptism; one God and Father of all, who is over all and through all and in all."

One body means "the church where Jesus Christ is the head." Just like you as a person have many parts that function together, such as arms, legs, feet, hands, eyes, and ears, the church, called the body of Christ, has many members who function as one church. The reference to the church is not referring to any denomination.

One Spirit is "the Holy Spirit of God, also called the Spirit of Christ, while the *One Lord* refers to Jesus Christ, the Son of God."

One faith means "trust and belief in God our Father, in Jesus Christ, His Son, and the Holy Spirit."

One baptism means "when you accept Jesus as your Lord and Savior, you become part of Jesus Christ." He lives within your spirit, baptizing you into Christ. This baptism is a spiritual baptism, which is very different from physical baptisms such as water baptism or infant baptism.

In Scripture, the capitalized word *God* usually refers to

"God, our Father," while the terms *Word, Lord,* or *Christ* refer to "God's Son, Jesus." Likewise, the capitalized word *Spirit* refers to "the Holy Spirit of God, sometimes referred to as the Holy Ghost." The reference to the Holy Ghost is not to be confused with any paranormal essence or activity. The Holy Spirit is the third member of the Trinity. Jesus always referred to the Holy Spirit with a masculine pronoun.

In the Old Testament, the people knew this three-in-one God by His revealed names. Let's look at a few of the many words:

Eloheim means "Mighty God, Creator of man and the universe, and sovereign God" (Genesis 1:1).

El Elyon means "Most High God, the highest authority in heaven and earth" (Genesis 14:18).

El Olam means "the eternal God or the everlasting God" (Genesis 21:33).

Adonai means "sovereign God, Master, or Lord God" (Genesis 15:2).

El Shaddai means "the Almighty God or All-Sufficient One. The God who is more than enough for every situation and need" (Genesis 17:1).

Jehovah Jirah means "Provider. The God who provides all of our needs" (Genesis 22:14).

Jehovah Rapha means "Healer. The God who heals all our sicknesses and diseases" (Exodus 15:26).

Jehovah Shalom means "God, our peace"—a name

used only once in the book of Judges (Judges 6:24).

Yahweh means "the Lord Jehovah," a word the Jewish people think of as too holy to mention; it is spelled "YHWH" (Genesis 2, Exodus 3).

These words describe who God is, but not His relationship with us. So, for example, when God created Adam and Eve, the Bible does not say they walked in the garden with God but that they recognized the voice of God as He walked in the garden in the cool of the day.

> *...they heard the sound of the Lord God walking in the garden in the cool of the day, and the man and his wife hid themselves from the presence of the Lord God among the trees of the garden. Then the Lord God called to the man, and said to him, "Where are you?" He said, "I heard the sound of You in the garden, and I was afraid because I was naked; so I hid..."*
>
> **Genesis 3:8–10 (NASB)**

God told Adam how to care for the garden. Then later, God revealed Himself as the God of Abraham, Isaac, and Jacob. Now, let us look at God, the Father, Jesus, the Son, and the Holy Spirit separately to understand who each of these three persons is.

CHAPTER 3:

WHO IS GOD—OUR FATHER?

The Bible, God's Word, tells us that *God is love*. Not only is His very nature love, but He also loves us as a Father loves His children, resulting in protection, goodness, and kindness toward us. You may not have had a father who loved you, or maybe he wasn't around for whatever reason, but Father God will always love you and never forsake you. So let us look at a few scriptures to see Him.

Second Corinthians 6:18 (NKJV), "I will be a Father to you, And you shall be My sons and daughters, Says the Lord Almighty."

First John 4:8 (NKJV), "...God is love."

First John 4:19 (NIV), "We love because he first loved us."

Romans 8:28 (NIV), "And we know that in all things God works for the good of those who love him, who have been called according to his purpose."

Father God is the source of our existence. He provides for us, corrects us, and loves us regardless of whether we love Him or not. His love is unchangeable; He seeks to work all things together for our good. He will never stop loving us and will not leave us. However, you and I can reject Him and separate ourselves from Him.

First John 3:1 (NKJV), "Behold what manner of love the Father has bestowed on us, that we should be called children of God!"

Jesus called God *Abba Father*. Abba is the Aramaic equivalent to our English word for father or papa; it speaks of a close, intimate, trusting relationship between a child and a loving father. It also recognizes a relationship of authority meant to protect. When Jesus was in the Garden of Gethsemane, He recognized His Father's power when He said, "All things are possible for you." He also trusted His Father enough to accept what was before Him. Look at Mark 14:36.

Mark 14:36 (NKJV), "And He said, 'Abba, Father, all things are possible for You. Take this cup away from Me; nevertheless, not what I will, but what You will.'"

What would it feel like to know God as your Abba Father? God is not angry or disappointed with you, but instead, He gathers you to Himself as His family—as His child. Nothing in this world can separate the love of God from you. Look what the apostle Paul had to say to the church in Rome.

Who shall separate us from the love of Christ?
Shall trouble or hardship or persecution or
famine or nakedness or danger or sword?
No, in all these things, we are more than
conquerors through him who loved us. For
I am convinced that neither death nor life,
neither angels nor demons, neither the present
nor the future, nor any powers, neither height
nor depth, nor anything else in all creation,
will be able to separate us from the love of
God that is in Christ Jesus our Lord.

Romans 8:35, 37–39 (NIV)

You need to understand that only sin, which is disobeying or ignoring God's Word, can separate you from God. Even if you sin, God will not separate you from His love. Instead, you separate yourself from your fellowship with God. You might ask, "What does that mean?" When you sin, you feel guilty or anxious over your choices. In your innermost being, you know you have done something not right, even if you do not know God's Word on the thing you have done. Sin is a choice you make, and it has consequences. Separation comes because God cannot look on or participate in sin. Do not despair—just repent and ask God to forgive you. The online Merriman-Webster Dictionary defines *repent* as "turning from sin, feeling regret and contrition."

You might ask, "What is sin?" If you go to the book of Exodus in the Old Testament, you find the commandments (Exodus 20:2–17) that God gave the children of Israel so they would be free from sin. If they followed the

39

commandments, they would be righteous in His eyes. We know them as the Ten Commandments.

You shall not have any other gods before Me.

You shall not make idols.

You shall not take the name of the Lord your God in vain.

Remember the Sabbath day and keep it holy.

Honor your father and mother.

You shall not murder.

You shall not commit adultery.

You shall not steal.

You shall not bear false witness against your neighbor.

You shall not covet your neighbors' stuff.

The problem was that the people could not keep them. If a person broke only one of the commandments, they had failed them all. In short, it was almost impossible to live by these rules. Spiritual death was the penalty for the sin of disobeying the commandments.

Romans 6:23 (NIV), "For the wages of sin is death, but the gift of God is eternal life in Christ Jesus our Lord."

Remember, sincerely repent, and ask God to forgive you if you feel separated from God because of your sin. He will forgive you immediately, and even in your sin, He never stops loving you!

> *For everyone has sinned; we all fall short*
> *of God's glorious standard. Yet God, in his*

grace, freely makes us right in his sight. He did this through Christ Jesus when he freed us from the penalty for our sins. For God presented Jesus as the sacrifice for sin. People are made right with God when they repent and believe that Jesus sacrificed his life, shedding his blood.

Romans 3:23–25 (NLT)

You need to know how sin came to be in the world. After God created the world and all within it, He created man. Let's go to Genesis 2:7.

Genesis 2:7 (NKJV), "And the Lord God formed man of the dust of the ground and breathed into his nostrils the breath of life, and man became a living being."

When God formed man from the dust of the ground, God breathed His very breath into humanity, making him human. Then God placed this man in a beautiful garden called the garden of Eden.

Then the Lord God took the man and put him in the garden of Eden to tend and keep it. And the Lord God commanded the man, saying, "Of every tree of the garden you may freely eat; but of the tree of the knowledge of good and evil you shall not eat, for in the day that you eat of it you shall surely die."

Genesis 2:15–17 (NKJV)

God gave Adam specific instructions: He could eat from every tree except the one in the center of the garden, "the tree of the knowledge of good and evil." Then God also saw that Adam needed a helper or a companion because none of the animals could fill that role for Adam.

Genesis 2:18 (NKJV), "And the Lord God said, 'It is not good that man should be alone; I will make him a helper comparable to him.'"

> *And the Lord God caused a deep sleep to fall on Adam, and he slept, and He took one of his ribs and closed up the flesh in its place. Then the rib which the Lord God had taken from man He made into a woman, and He brought her to the man. And Adam said: "This is now bone of my bones And flesh of my flesh; She shall be called Woman, Because she was taken out of Man."*

Genesis 2:21–23 (NKJV)

You know this woman by the name of Eve, Adam's wife. One day, the serpent, identified in the book of Revelation as Satan or the devil (Revelation 12:9, 20:2), appeared to her and said the forbidden tree's fruit was delicious, and she and Adam should eat some of it. After some discussion with the serpent, Eve ate some herself and offered some to Adam, which he ate. The serpent deceived Eve, but Adam disobeyed God's command not to eat the fruit. Disobedience to God is sin! When sin entered the world, it caused a separation between God and man. As a result, man's relationship and fellowship with God were broken.

But Father God, with His unquenchable love and mercy for humanity, began immediately to make a way to restore the relationship.

Romans 5:8–9 (NKJV), "But God demonstrates His own love toward us, in that while we were still sinners, Christ died for us. Much more then, having now been justified by His blood, we shall be saved from wrath through Him."

God had a plan! He would send Jesus Christ to the earth as a human being to demonstrate His love for us and show us the way back to Him. In the New Testament, God reveals Himself as the Father of the family.

CHAPTER 4:
WHO IS JESUS CHRIST?

Jesus Christ is the second person in the Trinity. He is not the Father nor the Holy Spirit. Instead, He is God, the Son, and is God in every way. Yet, even though He remained God, He laid aside His position as God to voluntarily come to the earth as a man to open the way for everyone to be set free from their sin and to show us the way to eternal life with God.

John 3:16–17 (NKJV), "For God so loved the world that He gave His only begotten Son, that whoever believes in Him should not perish but have everlasting life. For God did not send His Son into the world to condemn the world, but that the world through Him might be saved."

Jesus, the Son of God, came to us from heaven to show us the love of the Father and to save all of us from the doom and destruction caused by sin. He did not have to do this; Father God sent Jesus to us—you and me—out of His love for us. Let us see who the man Jesus is and how He came to our rescue.

In the beginning was the Word, and the Word was with God, and the Word was God. He was in the beginning with God. All things were made through Him, and without Him nothing was made that was made. In Him was life, and the life was the light of men. And the light shines in the darkness, and the darkness did not comprehend it.

John 1:1–5 (NKJV)

John 1:14, 17 (NKJV), "And the Word became flesh and dwelt among us, and we beheld His glory, the glory as of the only begotten of the Father, full of grace and truth. For the law was given through Moses, but grace and truth came through Jesus Christ."

But when the right time came, God sent his Son, born of a woman, subject to the law. God sent him to buy freedom for us who were slaves to the law so that he could adopt us as his very own children. And because we are his children, God has sent the Spirit of his Son into our hearts, prompting us to call out, "Abba, Father." Now, you are no longer a slave but God's child. And since you are his child, God has made you his heir.

Galatians 4:4–7 (NLT)

Father God sent His Son Jesus to earth to redeem you and restore your relationship and fellowship with Him at just the right time. Jesus loves you so much that if you had been the only person on earth, He still would have voluntarily left His heavenly home to come as a human being to rescue you. In addition, Jesus came to show you the Father's love, to forgive your sins, to give you abundant and everlasting life, and to intercede for you with the Father. He came to make sure you could be part of God's family as a child of God and show you how to have a close, intimate relationship with Father God, the Holy Spirit, and Himself. As you can see, Jesus came to earth as a human being even though He was entirely God. Jesus called Himself the Son of Man, identifying Himself with humanity (Matthew 18:11).

To understand more about Jesus, we need to begin with His birth.

In the sixth month of Elizabeth's pregnancy, God sent the angel Gabriel to Nazareth, a town in Galilee, to a virgin pledged to be married to a man named Joseph, a descendant of David. The virgin's name was Mary. The angel went to her and said, "Greetings, you who are highly favored! The Lord is with you." Mary was greatly troubled at his words and wondered what kind of greeting this might be. But the angel said to her, "Do not be afraid, Mary; you have found favor with God. You will conceive and give birth to a son, and you are to call him Jesus. He will be great and will be called the Son of the Most High. The Lord God will give him the throne of his father David, and he will reign over Jacob's descendants forever; his kingdom will never end." "How will this be," Mary asked the angel, "since I am a virgin?" The angel answered, "The Holy Spirit will come on you, and the power of the Most High will overshadow you. So the holy one to be born will be called the Son of God."

Luke 1:26–35 (NIV)

Every person was born of man's seed, making them a descendant of Adam, with his sinful nature. But Jesus' birth made Him a unique human being; He was born of a woman, not a man. How could this happen? Jesus was conceived by the power of God—the Holy Spirit. And because He was born of the Seed of God, He inherited the nature of God—the nature of love.

First John 4:8 (NIV), "…God is love."

Let's look more at Jesus' life and work while on earth. First, after His birth, we only hear of Him again when He was twelve years old at the temple in Jerusalem (Luke 2:46–49). Then, we see Him again as He began His ministry around the age of thirty, teaching people about His Father God and the kingdom of God for approximately three and a half years.

Luke 3:23 (NIV), "Now Jesus himself was about thirty years old when he began his ministry."

The religious leaders taught the Covenant of the Law, also known as the Ten Commandments, but they added many more rules that kept the people in bondage; however, Jesus taught the love and mercy of God, giving people hope for a better life. After some time, the religious leaders became angry because they had lost the power and authority they held over the people, so they determined to kill Jesus. He was declared guilty. The verdict was death by crucifixion.

Second Corinthians 5:21 (NLT), "For God made Christ, who never sinned, to be the offering for our sin, so that we could be made right with God through Christ."

Notice the scripture says that Father God willingly offered Jesus up to be crucified to pay for the sin debt we owed.

Luke 24:7 (NIV), "The Son of Man must be delivered over to the hands of sinners, be crucified and on the third day be raised again."

Romans 6:23 (NKJV), "For the wages of sin is death..."

Jesus was our substitute sacrifice. He was sinless but willingly died on a cross to deliver all people, including you, from your sin. As your substitute, God put all your sin on Jesus so that you could be sinless and righteous before Him. Sometimes, this is hard to understand, but God planned to have Jesus bear all the sin of the world, to redeem and restore all people to Himself—and that includes you. To be included in Jesus' sacrifice for your sin, you have to accept the gift that He gladly paid for you. You do this by accepting Jesus as your Savior and Lord. Let us continue.

When Jesus had been dead for three days and had paid the price for sin, the Holy Spirit of God raised Him from the dead. Then, forty days later, the disciples watched as Jesus ascended into heaven, where He sits at the right hand of Father God, in the seat of honor, where He intercedes for each of us.

Acts 1:9 (NIV), "After he said this, he was taken up before their very eyes, and a cloud hid him from their sight."

Before Jesus ascended to heaven, He told them He would prepare a place for them and come again to take them where He is. Look what He said about heaven.

> *"Don't let your hearts be troubled. Trust in God, and trust also in me. There is more than enough room in my Father's home. If this were not so, would I have told you that I will prepare a place for you? When everything is ready, I will come and get you, so that you will always be with me where I am. And you know the way to where I am going." "No, we don't know, Lord," Thomas said. "We have no idea where you are going, so how can we know the way?" Jesus told him, "I am the way, the truth, and the life. No one can come to the Father except through me. If you had really known me, you would know who my Father is. From now on, you do know him and have seen him!"*
>
> **John 14:1–7 (NLT)**

Jesus willingly took your sin on Himself to pay the price of death for you, then Jesus ascended into heaven. But before Jesus ascended into heaven, He told those watching that He would come back for them. So, if you are born again, Jesus is coming back for you too. In the meantime, He continues to intercede for you (Romans 8:34). *Intercede* means "to pray or petition on behalf of another" (Schaff 1996, 102). Can you comprehend God's Son, Jesus Christ, praying for you? Even though Jesus is in heaven, He said He would never leave you nor forsake you. Therefore, He continuously prays for you because He loves and values you.

Deuteronomy 31:8 (NIV), "The Lord himself goes before you and will be with you; he will never leave you nor forsake you. Do not be afraid; do not be discouraged."

First Peter 5:7 (NIV), "Cast all your anxiety on him because he cares for you."

Hebrews 4:16 (NIV), "Let us then approach God's throne of grace with confidence so that we may receive mercy and find grace to help us in our time of need."

One of my favorite verses is Hebrews 4:16 because it comforts me to know I can approach God my Father, Jesus, or the Holy Spirit with any concern I have. I approach Him knowing that He will hear and answer me. You can have that same assurance. Let us go back to continue our study of who Jesus is.

In addition to everything we have learned so far, Jesus showed us how to know our Father God. I do not know about you, but for me, that is a great big *Wow*! Think about it; you can know God—the Creator of the universe! Not just about Him but have a relationship with Him. You can talk to Him anytime you choose, and then He answers you—but you have to actively listen with your spiritual ears. God gave you Jesus, who is also called the Word of God, the written Word of God that you can read for yourself. As you read His Word, you will know Him more and more. When you know Jesus, you can understand Father God's nature and love for you. Listen to what Jesus said about Himself and the Father God:

John 10:30 (NKJV), "I and My Father are one."

John 14:6–7 (NLT), "Jesus told him, 'I am the way, the truth, and the life. No one can come to the Father except through me. If you had really known me, you would know who my Father is. From now on, you do know him and have seen him!'"

John 14:9 (NIV), "Anyone who has seen me has seen the Father."

Look what Jesus said about Himself using objects you can understand.

John 6:35 (NIV), "Then Jesus declared, 'I am the bread of life. Whoever comes to me will never go hungry, and whoever believes in me will never be thirsty.'"

John 4:10 (NLT), "Jesus replied, 'If you only knew the gift God has for you and who you are speaking to, you would ask me, and I would give you living water.'"

Every culture in the world eats bread and drinks water to sustain physical life. Jesus is not only the *Bread of Life*, but He is also the *Living Water* that you need to support your spiritual life.

Jesus is the light of the world. Without light, there is only darkness. The darkness can be actual physical darkness, spiritual darkness, intellectual darkness, or emotional darkness. Jesus is speaking of spiritual darkness. In the online Merriam-Webster Dictionary, one definition of *darkness* is "a lack of knowledge or enlightenment." The light Jesus is talking about is understanding or knowledge. I like to say, "You cannot know what you do not know." When you know something or someone, you understand that person or thing.

John 8:12 (NLT), "Jesus spoke to the people once more and said, 'I am the light of the world. If you follow me, you won't have to walk in darkness, because you will have the light that leads to life.'"

Light is also knowledge. Knowledge reveals truth and understanding. Even though Jesus was speaking to the Jews, the principle is the same today. His Word is a beacon of light or wisdom that reveals absolute truth, giving freedom.

John 8:31–32 (NLT), "Jesus said to the people who believed in him, 'You are truly my disciples if you remain faithful to my teachings. And you will know the truth, and the truth will set you free.'"

God's Word shines a light on the truth, so we do not have to wonder what is true or false. Truth sets us free, while lies and half-truths keep us in bondage and darkness.

Jesus is the door. A room or chamber has a doorway that allows entrance. In this case, Jesus is the door for us to enter the section called heaven and the presence of God.

John 10:7 (NKJV), "Then Jesus said to them again, 'Most assuredly, I say to you, I am the door of the sheep.'"

Jesus is the Good Shepherd. A good shepherd looks after and protects the sheep of his flock. If necessary, the shepherd will die to protect them. Jesus has already died on the cross for you—a sheep in His pasture. People are called sheep in various places in the Scriptures; the character of sheep is interesting in that they have a gentle nature and are usually obedient to their shepherd. When you are obedient to your Shepherd, Jesus, He becomes your leader and protector.

John 10:14–15 (NKJV), "I am the good shepherd; I know My sheep and am known by My own. As the Father knows Me, even so I know the Father; and I lay down My life for the sheep."

Psalm 95:7 (NIV), "For he is our God and we are the people of his pasture, the flock under his care."

His pasture is a picture of His presence, where you can find peace, rest, and comfort. He is the Shepherd, and you are His sheep. Like a sheep, you can let Him have control of your life, knowing He will protect you.

Jesus is an apostle. As an apostle, Jesus represents God to man and man to God. An apostle is similar to an ambassador, a person authorized to represent a higher authority or government on a particular assignment. Nations throughout the world send ambassadors to other nations to represent their country, making sure their interests are protected. So Jesus, the apostle, represents you to the Father.

> *And so, dear brothers and sisters who belong*
> *to God and are partners with those called*
> *to heaven, think carefully about this Jesus*
> *whom we declare to be God's messenger*
> *and High Priest. For he was faithful to God,*
> *who appointed him, just as Moses served*
> *faithfully when he was entrusted with God's*
> *entire house. But Jesus deserves far more*
> *glory than Moses, just as a person who builds*
> *a house deserves more praise than the house*
> *itself. For every house has a builder, but the*
> *one who built everything is God. Moses was*
> *certainly faithful in God's house as a servant.*
> *His work was an illustration of the truths*
> *God would reveal later. But Christ, as the*
> *Son, is in charge of God's entire house. And*
> *we are God's house, if we keep our courage*
> *and remain confident in our hope in Christ.*
>
> **Hebrews 3:1–6 (NLT)**

Jesus is the high priest. As the high priest, Jesus atoned
for your sin; He paid the ultimate price by shedding His
blood, not the blood of animals. However, Jesus shed His
blood only once for your sin. He never has to shed His
blood again. Because of His blood, you can go boldly to
the throne of grace whenever you need help or only want
to praise or worship God for all your blessings.

> *So then, since we have a great High Priest who*
> *has entered heaven, Jesus the Son of God, let*
> *us hold firmly to what we believe. This High*
> *Priest of ours understands our weaknesses,*

*for he faced all of the same testings we do,
yet he did not sin. So let us come boldly to
the throne of our gracious God. There we will
receive his mercy, and we will find grace to
help us when we need it most.*

Hebrews 4:14–16 (NLT)

Jesus is the resurrection and life. When a person believes in and accepts Jesus Christ as Lord, that person receives eternal life. To have eternal life means to dwell in the presence of God now and forever. The online Merriam-Webster Dictionary defines *eternal* as "having infinite duration, valid or existing at all times, and ageless." So eternal life in Christ begins when you accept Jesus as your Savior.

John 3:36 (NIV), "Whoever believes in the Son has eternal life…"

John 5:24 (NIV), "Very truly I tell you, whoever hears my word and believes him who sent me has eternal life and will not be judged but has crossed over from death to life."

John 11:25–26 (NKJV), "Jesus said to her, 'I am the resurrection and the life. He who believes in Me, though he may die, he shall live. And whoever lives and believes in Me shall never die. Do you believe this?'"

John 10:10 (NKJV), "I have come that they may have life, and that they may have it more abundantly."

Some people may argue that abundant life only means natural life as we live on this planet. That might be true, but consider this, "If you have eternal life in the presence of God, would not that also qualify you for abundant life when you join Him in heaven?"

Jesus is the way. He is the only way to the Father, and He is not only truthful, but He is truth itself, and in Him, there is eternal life—an everlasting life that can only come when you join Him in heaven.

John 14:6 (NKJV), "Jesus said to him, 'I am the way, the truth, and the life. No one comes to the Father except through Me.'"

Jesus is the healer. Everywhere Jesus went, He healed the sick and afflicted. So Jesus is your healer too.

Matthew 4:23 (NKJV), "And Jesus went about all Galilee, teaching in their synagogues, preaching the gospel of the kingdom, and healing all kinds of sickness and all kinds of disease among the people."

Luke 4:40 (NIV), "At sunset, the people brought to Jesus all who had various kinds of sickness, and laying his hands on each one, he healed them."

We have only looked at a few of Jesus' names. There are many more names in the Bible that you can explore.

CHAPTER 5:

WHO IS THE HOLY SPIRIT?

The Holy Spirit is God, the third member of the Trinity. He is also called the *Spirit of Christ* and has other names as well. He is not the Father nor Jesus the Son but is God. After Jesus' death and resurrection, as Jesus was preparing His disciples for His return to heaven, He spoke to them about the Holy Spirit. The Helper who would come as an advocate and comforter. Twelve times, Jesus used the masculine pronoun *He* or *Him* to refer to the Holy Spirit, which tells you the Holy Spirit is a person, not a paranormal experience, a ghost, or a thing. He is the *Spirit of God*.

The number *twelve* in the Bible symbolizes God's power and authority; twelve means perfection or completeness.

> *But very truly I tell you, it is for your good that I am going away. Unless I go away, the Advocate will not come to you; but I will send him to you if I go. When he comes, he will*

prove the world to be in the wrong about sin and righteousness and judgment: about sin, because people do not believe in me; about righteousness, because I am going to the Father, where you can see me no longer; and about judgment, because the prince of this world now stands condemned.

"I have much more to say to you, more than you can now bear. But when he, the Spirit of truth, comes, he will guide you into all the truth. He will not speak on his own; he will speak only what he hears, and he will tell you what is yet to come. He will glorify me because it is from me that he will receive what he will make known to you. All that belongs to the Father is mine. That is why I said the Spirit will receive from me what he will make known to you."

John 16:7–15 (NIV)

The Scriptures tell us that the Holy Spirit was just as active in creating the world and man as God our Father and Jesus Christ.

Genesis 1:1–2 (NIV), "In the beginning God created the heavens and the earth. Now the earth was formless and empty, darkness was over the surface of the deep, and the Spirit of God was hovering over the waters."

He was part of the *design team* that put the world in place with its differences and complexities. *As the breath of life*, He breathed life into Adam and Eve.

The Holy Spirit is the power of God that overshadowed

Mary to bring forth the God-man Jesus as a human being (Luke 1:31–35).

When Jesus was near the time of His death, as He was preparing the disciples for when He would no longer be with them, He announced that the Father would send another Helper to them, but they did not understand.

> *If you love Me, keep My commandments. And I will pray the Father, and He will give you another Helper, that He may abide with you forever—the Spirit of truth, whom the world cannot receive, because it neither sees Him nor knows Him; but you know Him, for He dwells with you and will be in you.*
>
> **John 14:15–17 (NKJV)**

In this verse, Jesus told His disciples that the Helper, referring to the Holy Spirit, would come and live in and with them forever, even though they would not see Him. The Holy Spirit lives in every person who has accepted Jesus Christ as their Savior and Lord.

The message "the Holy Spirit is living in you, but you will not see Him" might sound confusing, so look at a couple of examples. One example would be that you cannot see the wind when it blows, but you can see the effects of the wind blowing. Another example would be an explosion. You can hear the sound of the blast, and you might be able to see the items used to trigger the explosion, but you cannot see the power that caused the explosion. Another example would be turning on an electric light. When you turn on a light, you can see the change from darkness to light, but you cannot see the electrical power that caused the light to turn on. The Holy Spirit is the power of God in action. That power lives in everyone who has accepted Jesus Christ as their Lord and Savior.

Jesus made sure the disciples would know exactly who the Holy Spirit was, where He came from, and what He would do for everyone on earth. How will the Holy Spirit help you? Study the following scriptures to see how He can help you.

John 14:26 (NASB), "But the Helper, the Holy Spirit, whom the Father will send in My name, He will teach you all things, and bring to your remembrance all that I said to you."

John 15:26 (NASB), "When the Helper comes, whom I will send to you from the Father, that is the Spirit of truth who proceeds from the Father, He will testify about Me."

John 16:13 (NASB), "But when He, the Spirit of truth, comes, He will guide you into all the truth; for He will not speak on His own initiative, but whatever He hears, He will speak; and He will disclose to you what is to come."

The disciples were still distressed about Jesus leaving them; therefore, He told them it was to their advantage that He was going. So, likewise, it is to your advantage that Jesus returned to heaven too. Then the Holy Spirit can live in you as a born-again believer in Jesus Christ.

> *But I tell you the truth, it is to your advantage*
> *that I go away; for if I do not go away,*
> *the Helper will not come to you; but if I go,*

I will send Him to you. And He, when He comes, will convict the world concerning sin and righteousness and judgment; concerning sin, because they do not believe in Me; and concerning righteousness, because I go to the Father and you no longer see Me; and concerning judgment, because the ruler of this world has been judged.

John 16:7–11 (NASB)

Some translations use the word *Counselor* or *Advocate* instead of *Helper* when telling us about the Holy Spirit. The words *Counselor* and *Advocate* mean the same as *Helper.* The word *Counselor*, in Greek, is #3875 *Parakiētos*, meaning "to call to one's side as a legal advisor, pleader, proxy, or advocate, one who comes forward in behalf of, and as the representative of another" (Zodhiates 1984, 1718).

First John 2:1 (NKJV), "My little children, these things I write to you, so that you may not sin. And if anyone sins, we have an Advocate with the Father, Jesus Christ the righteous."

The Hebrew-Greek Key Study Bible tells us:

The Holy Spirit is designated by Jesus Christ as equal with himself as God. Therefore, the new Paraclete, the Holy Spirit was to witness concerning Jesus Christ and to glorify Him. The Holy Spirit is called a Paraclete because he is Christ's substitute on earth while Christ is away from the world. This word must not be understood as being applied to the Holy Spirit in the same sense as to Christ Jesus

63

> *where it is used with the meaning of our*
> *substitutionary advocate, but rather as He*
> *who pleads God's cause with us.*

Zodhiates 1984, 1718

The Holy Spirit is not only your helper, counselor, and advocate, but He is also your teacher. As God, the Holy Spirit knows the mind of God and is working in you to help you understand what God's will is for your life. The Holy Spirit is also known as the *Spirit of Truth*, and He will guide you into the truth in every part of your life if you listen to His small, soft voice. So just as you can have an intimate relationship with your heavenly Father and Jesus, you can also know and have a close relationship with the Holy Spirit.

In the Old Testament, the Spirit of God dwelled in the holy of holies in the Wilderness Tabernacle and later in the temple. The power of the Holy Spirit came upon specific people to give them a message from God for themselves, the people, or to anoint people for services such as the priests, prophets, and kings. Today the Spirit of God dwells in those who are believers in Jesus Christ. The apostle Paul also tells you that you are the temple of the Holy Spirit.

First Corinthians 3:16 (NKJV), "Do you not know that you are the temple of God and that the Spirit of God dwells in you?"

It is almost mind-blogging to consider that the Holy Spirit of God, the third person of the Trinity, lives in us. But just as the Wilderness Tabernacle and the temple had a Most Holy Place, there is a secret place in every born-again believer where the Holy Spirit dwells. When you choose by faith to believe in Jesus, you become the temple of the Holy Spirit—He lives in you. You can know the power of God in you. The power of living a life pleasing to God, a life that wants to know Him more. You can have a life filled with the joy of the Lord, where the concerns and the worries of this world have no power over you. Your life becomes not less with God but rather more—even to overflowing with His love. Then you will know the power of the secret place.

Psalm 91:1–2 (NLT), "Those who live in the shelter of the Most High will find rest in the shadow of the Almighty. This I declare about the Lord: He alone is my refuge, my place of safety; he is my God, and I trust him."

You cannot see the Holy Spirit, but you can see His work in signs that symbolize His presence. As you learn about these signs, you will be able to follow the workings and anointing of the Holy Spirit.

The Holy Spirit as a dove. The Holy Spirit appeared as a gentle dove anointing Jesus when He was baptized by John the Baptist at the Jordan River (John 1:29–33). The Holy Spirit appeared as a dove representing God's blessings, gentleness, purity, and patience with all people.

The Holy Spirit as tongues of fire. On the day of Pentecost, the Holy Spirit appeared as tongues of fire on the heads of those in the upper room, anointing them for service (Acts 2:2–4). Since then, every believer has been called to the ministry of reconciliation (2 Corinthians 5:18).

This means telling others about Jesus so they can be part of the family of God.

God's fire can also purify and refine you; it warms you, sanctifies you, and anoints you with a passion for praising and worshiping God.

The Holy Spirit brings joy. On the day of Pentecost, the Holy Spirit's outpouring brought so much joy to the people in the upper room that the bystanders thought they were drunk on wine. The apostle Peter explained that they were not drunk but filled with the Holy Spirit (Acts 2:15–17). From that time, those serving Jesus were filled with joy and saw many miracles as they preached the gospel of Jesus Christ.

The Holy Spirit as oil. Oil is another symbol of the Holy Spirit, symbolizing the anointing for ministry. In the Old Testament, a special anointing oil made from pure olive oil and specific spices was used to anoint the prophets, priests, and kings. The prophets offered comfort, instruction, and correction to the people. The priests worshiped God for themselves and the people, while the kings led and governed them. When the anointing of the Holy Spirit is on you, you receive supernatural direction, words, and abilities beyond what is natural, never something you can make happen—it is always the Holy Spirit.

The wind is another sign of the Holy Spirit. The Holy Spirit comes like the wind, symbolizing His power and guidance. On the day of Pentecost, the people heard the sound of a rushing wind (Acts 2:2). The people didn't see the wind but listened to its sound. The Holy Spirit is like the wind, you cannot see Him, but the results are evident.

The Holy Spirit is symbolized by water. Water symbolizes the cleansing that occurs in the new birth of a person when they accept Jesus Christ as their Savior. No one can enter the kingdom of God without being born of water and the Spirit (John 3:5). Water also quenches thirst. Jesus said that if you drink the water He gives you, you will never thirst again (John 4:13–14).

Clothing also symbolizes the Holy Spirit. We see this when Jesus told the disciples to wait in Jerusalem to be *clothed* with power from the Holy Spirit (Luke 24:49).

The Holy Spirit is manifest as fruit. The Holy Spirit not only teaches you but produces fruit in you. As believers in Jesus Christ, the fruit of the Spirit is produced in you as you mature spiritually. This fruit is the manifestation of the Spirit of God in you. All you do is bear the fruit like an apple tree bears apples. The prophet Hosea said the fruit is from the Lord (Hosea 14:8). Then the apostle Paul defined the fruit of the Spirit in Galatians chapter 5.

Galatians 5:22–23 (NLT), "But the Holy Spirit produces this kind of fruit in our lives: love, joy, peace, patience, kindness, goodness, faithfulness, gentleness, and self-control."

Jesus told His disciples that bearing fruit was necessary, and unless they remained faithful to Him, they would not bear fruit. Notice that only the Holy Spirit can produce the fruit, and only you can bear the fruit.

Remain in me, as I also remain in you. No

> *branch can bear fruit by itself; it must remain in the vine. Neither can you bear fruit unless you remain in me. "I am the vine; you are the branches. If you remain in me and I in you, you will bear much fruit; apart from me you can do nothing. If you do not remain in me, you are like a branch that is thrown away and withers; such branches are picked up, thrown into the fire and burned. If you remain in me and my words remain in you, ask whatever you wish, and it will be done for you. This is to my Father's glory, that you bear much fruit, showing yourselves to be my disciples."*
>
> **John 15:4–8 (NIV)**

It is important to understand that Jesus is not talking about multiple fruits but one fruit. That one fruit is manifest in nine different ways. Another way to understand this is to picture an orange or grapefruit. You have only one orange or grapefruit, but there are many slices or segments in that one fruit when peeled.

If you study the purpose of the fruit of the Spirit, you will find several ways of looking at it. I like to picture the fruit in three groups.

The first group is love, joy, and peace. The first three fruits mentioned are God's spiritual forces: God our Father is love, the Holy Spirit brings us joy, and Jesus is our peace. As we mature in the knowledge of God, we become more like Him. The love of the Father, the joy of the Holy Spirit, and the peace of Jesus Christ become our standard for living.

The next group is patience, kindness, and goodness. These three fruits are how you are to interact with each other. Be patient, treating others with compassion and integrity. Jesus told us how to treat others.

> *As the Father loved Me, I also have loved you; abide in My love. If you keep My commandments, you will abide in My love, just as I have kept My Father's commandments and abide in His love.*

> *These things I have spoken to you, that My joy may remain in you, and that your joy may be full. This is My commandment, that you love one another as I have loved you. Greater love has no one than this, than to lay down one's life for his friends.*

John 15:9–13 (NKJV)

It takes the fruit of the Spirit to love as Jesus loved you. When this fruit is evident in your life, you have learned to walk in the same love that God has for you.

In the final group, faithfulness, gentleness, and self-control are the fruits only you can display. Ask yourself, "Am I faithful to the Lord? Am I gentle in my everyday interactions with others, and do I have self-control?" These fruits are displayed when no one is watching.

When I was about eight or nine years old, our pastor talked to us before going to Children's Church on Sundays. One day, He asked, "If Jesus came to visit you today, would He be pleased to see what you are doing or where you are?" That was said to me many years ago, and

I have not forgotten it. I believe that question kept me from doing things I might have done that I shouldn't have. Things that were not pleasing to God or my parents. How will you answer that question? I know a similar slogan, "What would Jesus do?" surfaced several years ago, and it bears repeating. That slogan actually asked what Jesus would do, but the questions are, "What are *you* doing?" and "Will God be pleased by *your* actions?"

The fruit of the Spirit contrasts with the fruit of the flesh, which Paul cautions us to avoid in Galatians 5. The works of the flesh bring division and heartbreak, while the fruit of the Spirit brings unity and harmony into your life.

We have learned who God is. He is God, the Father, God the Son, Jesus Christ, and God the Holy Spirit. Let us see how they work together by looking at the Glory Circle— I'm not sure where I first saw this, but it is something I've never forgotten. It shows us how God works together on our behalf.

The Father glorifies the Son as the only way to the heart of God.

The Son lives to glorify the Father by constantly seeking to reconcile us and all things to the Father.

The Holy Spirit glorifies the Son and the Father by dwelling in us, giving us the power to obey the Father and faith to trust the Son, and the Holy Spirit gives us the ability to witness and minister to others. This power demonstrates God's love and willingness to help all people.

Finally, God is one God—in three persons, not three

gods. He is Almighty God, the God of all creation, and now with the Holy Spirit, He reveals Himself as the indwelling God. If you have accepted Jesus as your Savior and Lord, the Holy Spirit lives in you. The same attributes and characteristics belong to God as a whole—Father God, Jesus Christ, and the Holy Spirit. They are one and work together in unity, each having different functions. Let us learn about those characteristics and attributes.

CHAPTER 6:

WHAT ARE GOD'S CHARACTERISTICS?

By identifying some of God's characteristics, you can understand who God is. For example, trusting someone only comes when you know that person; therefore, knowing God will help you trust Him and determine who you are.

God is an eternal Spirit, invisible, immaterial, and everlasting. Even though Jesus walked on earth as a human being with a physical body, He now resides in heaven with Father God. The Holy Spirit lives in all born-again believers.

John 4:24 (NKJV), "God is Spirit, and those who worship Him must worship in spirit and truth."

The word *Spirit* in verse 24 means "that which is beyond physical or material."

Second Corinthians 3:17 (NIV), "Now the Lord is

the Spirit, and where the Spirit of the Lord is, there is freedom."

The online Merriam-Webster Dictionary defines *eternal* and *eternity* as "something which has infinite duration, everlasting." *Eternal* means "endless, having no beginning and no end in time." Eternity exists at all times and is forever and always accurate or valid. Eternity is yesterday, today, and forever, without beginning or end. As an eternal God, He always has been and always will be.

Numbers 23:19 (NKJV), "God is not a man, that He should lie, Nor a son of man, that He should repent. Has He said, and will He not do? Or has He spoken, and will He not make it good?"

In this scripture, we learn that God cannot lie. The online Merriam-Webster Dictionary defines *lie* as "to make an untrue, false, or a misleading statement with the intent to deceive someone. To make an inaccurate statement that may or may not be true by the speaker is also a lie." Proverbs 6 also tells us that God hates lying, among other things.

> *These six things the Lord hates,*
> *Yes, seven are an abomination to Him:*
> *A proud look,*
> *A lying tongue,*
> *Hands that shed innocent blood,*
> *A heart that devises wicked plans,*
> *Feet that are swift in running to evil,*

A false witness who speaks lies,

And one who sows discord among brethren.

Proverbs 6:16–19 (NKJV)

The apostle Paul also tells us that God cannot and does not lie! Therefore, His word is true and can be trusted.

Titus is a letter from the apostle Paul to Titus, a young Greek believer, telling Titus who Paul was and his message to believers.

> *I have been sent to proclaim faith to those God has chosen and to teach them to know the truth that shows them how to live godly lives. This truth gives them confidence that they have eternal life, which God—who does not lie—promised them before the world began.*

Titus 1:1–2 (NLT)

In today's world, you experience lies, untruths, and false or misleading statements so often that sometimes, you do not know who or what to believe. Most people are honest, yet a seemingly harmless lie is the usual way of life for some people. The Scriptures tell us that God hates lies! If you have to lie to keep from hurting someone, it is better to be still and say nothing. If you are a person who lies, no matter how big or little, ask God to forgive you and help you not lie anymore. He will do it!

God is love. There are several types of love. Most people understand love as conditional love: if you do this, I will do that. God's love is different, and it is unconditional. His love is a supernatural, spiritual force that defies human nature. His love acts without any expectation of return, but when you know that God loves you, you cannot help but declare your love for Him.

Jeremiah 31:3 (NIV), "The Lord appeared to us in the past, saying:

"'I have loved you with an everlasting love;

"'I have drawn you with unfailing kindness.'"

First John 4:9–10 (NIV), "This is how God showed his love among us: He sent his one and only Son into the world that we might live through him. This is love: not that we loved God, but that he loved us and sent his Son as an atoning sacrifice for our sins."

In Psalm 91 and John 3:16, God tells you what He will do because you love Him.

> *"Because he loves me," says the Lord, "I will rescue him;*
>
> *I will protect him, for he acknowledges my name.*
>
> *He will call on me, and I will answer him;*
>
> *I will be with him in trouble,*
>
> *I will deliver him and honor him.*
>
> *With long life I will satisfy him*
>
> *and show him my salvation."*
>
> **Psalm 91:14–16 (NIV)**

John 3:16–17 (NKJV), "For God so loved the world that He gave His only begotten Son, that whoever believes in Him should not perish but have everlasting life. For God did not send His Son into the world to condemn the world, but that the world through Him might be saved."

A few years ago, I was part of a team holding a Christian Ladies Conference in Moscow, Russia. One day while traveling on a subway, a friend pointed out an advertisement of John 3:16 printed in Russian. I could not speak, read, write, or understand Russian; I needed an interpreter. That evening, I had dinner at a table with five Russian ladies attending the conference. I wanted to talk with them, but there was not an interpreter available. Then I remembered the scripture John 3:16 that I had seen earlier that day on the subway advertisement. I looked up the Scripture in my English Bible and showed it to the lady sitting next to me because she could speak a little English. She immediately turned to the Scripture in her Russian Bible and shared it with the other ladies. We continued communicating this way for the remainder of the meal. As I was leaving the table to begin my evening conference duties, our young Russian server came to the table, and I heard her ask, in Russian, "Who is the 'Americano'?" She wanted to know what we were doing and why I was in Russia. One of the ladies began speaking to her about the conference. After the service, the ladies at the table came with an interpreter to tell me about their conversation with the young woman. The lady I had heard speaking with the young woman told her about the conference and Jesus. The server told them she was Jewish and did not need Jesus. The lady talking to her was a Jewish Christian and began to share about herself as a Jew and that she needed Jesus in her own life. She went on to tell the young woman that Jesus could be her Savior and Lord and that Jesus loved her. She told the young woman that she could know Jesus and His great love for her. I do not know the outcome of their discussion with her, but I know that God singled out that young woman that evening to tell her how much He loves her. If you are reading this book, perhaps God has singled you out today to tell you how much He loves you or to teach you how to share His love with others.

Whether you are a long-time believer or a new believer, Jesus wants to have a loving relationship with you. So He shows you His love every day in many ways. Most of the time, you might not even recognize His love. Stop for a moment and consider some life events where you experienced joy and happiness. Could this be God showing you His love? How about on a sunny day after several rainy days or on rainy days when we need rain? How about when you receive an unexpected gift or find a great bargain? How about beautiful flowers and trees or the colors of a rainbow? Or the beauty of the ocean or the majesty of the mountains? Or the delight experienced with kittens and puppies? Or the birth of a precious baby? How about an unexpected visit from a friend when you are hurting or lonely? God's love for you knows no boundaries and always knows what you want and need most. Everyone wants and needs love. Only God's love satisfies this most profound need. People love you conditionally, while God loves you unconditionally. And He loves you despite yourself. There is an old but true saying that "God loves us warts and all." That is true! Nothing will ever cause God to stop loving you. Look what the Scriptures say.

First Corinthians 13:8 (NKJV), "Love never fails."

> *No, in all these things we are more than conquerors through him who loved us. For I am convinced that neither death nor life, neither angels nor demons, neither the present nor the future, nor any powers, neither height nor depth, nor anything else in all creation, will be able to separate us from the love of God that is in Christ Jesus our Lord.*
>
> **Romans 8:37–39 (NIV)**

Paul teaches five things that will never keep God's love from you. They are:

1. *Death nor life*. Death is not to be feared. Consider what Paul told the believers in the church at Corinth regarding the secret of death.

> *I declare to you, brothers and sisters, that flesh and blood cannot inherit the kingdom of God, nor does the perishable inherit the imperishable. Listen, I tell you a mystery: We will not all sleep, but we will be changed— in a flash, in the twinkling of an eye, at the last trumpet. For the trumpet will sound, the dead will be raised imperishable, and we will be changed. For the perishable must clothe*

itself with the imperishable, and the mortal with immortality.

1 Corinthians 15:50–53 (NIV)

When I went into heaven, I stood before the Lord Jesus. He is so beautiful, and the atmosphere in heaven is beyond description, so there is no reason to fear death. As a believer in Jesus, when you leave this world, you will be in the presence of God for all eternity. Paul was correct in saying that death will not separate you from God's love. Even the trials of life cannot keep you from the love of God. Jesus said He came to give you life and a more abundant life.

John 10:10 (NKJV), "I have come that they may have life and that they may have it more abundantly."

2. *Neither angels, principalities, nor powers* can separate you from God's love. God created angels subject to Him and His love, so they must act with love—they cannot separate you from God or His love. In this verse, other angels, principalities, and powers are fallen angels and demons that Satan controls. They will do anything to try and separate you from God's love, but they cannot. Jesus took all power and dominion away from Satan; therefore, Satan and his demons have no control over you. However, you may choose to give them control instead of resisting them. James, the half-brother of Jesus, told you how to resist Satan, also known as the devil.

James 4:7–8 (NKJV), "Therefore submit to God.

Resist the devil and he will flee from you. Draw near to God and He will draw near to you."

If you belong to Jesus, you have the power to resist the demonic forces that try to capture your thinking and senses, the same forces that attempt to move you away from God. Many people deny that these forces are present in our world today, but all you need to do is look around you to see the evidence of sin and evil. For example, you can see evil when there is rioting and violence in the streets or when murders and senseless killings are running rampant. Another form of sin is the hatred prevalent at work in our society, especially on social media, which causes strife and more hate. Hate is not from God because He is love. James told us to resist the devil and evil and submit to God. When you submit to God, you draw near Him by staying in His Word and being obedient to Him—then sin has to flee.

3. *Neither things present nor things to come* can separate you from God's love. This scripture tells you that the past is the past, and it cannot affect the love God has for you, and neither can anything in the future separate you from God's love. Look at what the prophet Isaiah and the apostle Paul had to say about the past:

   Isaiah 43:18 (NKJV), "Do not remember the former things, nor consider the things of old."

Not that I have already attained, or am already perfected; but I press on, that I may lay hold of that for which Christ Jesus has also laid hold of me. Brethren, I do not count myself to have apprehended; but one thing I do, forgetting those things which are behind and reaching forward to those things which are ahead, I press toward the goal for the prize of the upward call of God in Christ Jesus.

Philippians 3:12–14 (NKJV)

Paul told those in his time, and you, to forget the past and reach toward the goal of knowing Christ Jesus more and more. You cannot live on the glories of the past. Neither can you hold on to your regrettable past. Instead, ask God to forgive you, forgive yourself, and leave it in your past.

4. *Neither height nor depth* can separate you from God's love. You could go from the highest heaven, descend into the very core of the earth, or even to the outermost rim of space, and you would never be separated from God's love. Look what King David said in Psalm 139.

> *Where can I go from your Spirit?*
> *Where can I flee from your presence?*
> *If I go up to the heavens, you are there;*
> *if I make my bed in the depths, you are there.*
> *If I rise on the wings of the dawn,*
> *if I settle on the far side of the sea,*

even there your hand will guide me,

your right hand will hold me fast.

If I say, "Surely the darkness will hide me

and the light become night around me,"

even the darkness will not be dark to you;

the night will shine like the day,

for darkness is as light to you.

Psalm 139:7–12 (NIV)

5. *Nor any other created thing or object.* God is the Creator of all things. He took nothing and made something of value. You may take what He has designed and create something new, but His love will never depart from you. Have you ever considered how much God loves you? Previously, we spoke about this briefly, but let us look at it again because it is important. Remember Jesus came to show you the Father's love.

John 13:34 (NKJV), "A new commandment I give to you, that you love one another; as I have loved you, that you also love one another."

He never stops loving you. So each day when you wake up, tell Him you love Him. You don't have to "feel" loved to tell Him. Just do it! And watch how your day changes. God is good all the time!

I like to ask, "How much did Jesus love you?" The answer is that He gave up everything in heaven to come to earth to give you an abundant life on earth with eternal life in His presence when you leave this earth.

In the book of Exodus, we find the Exodus story with Moses as their leader. For more than four hundred years, the children of Israel were treated harshly as slaves by the Egyptians. Let us see what happened.

Moses was a Hebrew by birth, but He grew up in Pharaoh's court as the Pharaoh's daughter's son. His education and training were the finest available. However, when Moses was about forty years old, he killed an Egyptian who was mistreating a Hebrew slave. To avoid punishment by death, Moses ran to the desert of Midian, where he married Zipporah and had two sons, Gershom and Eliezer. Moses spent his time watching over his father-in-law Jethro's sheep and lived a quiet life for another forty years. Then, one day, God appeared to Moses in a burning bush, telling him that he was chosen to lead the Hebrew people out of Egypt (Exodus chapters 1–4).

Using Moses as a leader, God moved the children of Israel out of Egypt. Through Moses, God instructed the people how to live as God's special people and form the nation of Israel. Sometime later, God told Moses that He was pleased with him and knew him by name. Then, Moses asked God to show him His face; instead, God showed Moses His goodness.

And the Lord said to Moses, "I will do the very thing you have asked, because I am pleased with you and I know you by name." Then Moses said, "Now show me your glory." And the Lord said, "I will cause all my goodness to pass in front of you, and I will proclaim my name, the Lord, in your presence. I will have mercy on whom I will have mercy, and I will have compassion on whom I will have compassion. But," he said, "you cannot see my face, for no one may see me and live."

Exodus 33:17–20 (NIV)

God is good. According to the online Merriam-Webster dictionary, being *good* means being "kind, agreeable, and pleasant." God shows you His goodness every day in many ways. So think about all the goodness in your life— it comes from God.

Good and upright is the Lord;

therefore he instructs sinners in his ways.

He guides the humble in what is right

and teaches them his way.

All the ways of the Lord are loving and faithful

toward those who keep the demands of his covenant.

Psalm 25:8–10 (NIV)

Sometimes, when I need to remember that God is good to me all the time, I only have to look around to see His goodness in my life. He is good to you too.

Psalm 27:13 (NKJV), "I would have lost heart unless I had believed That I would see the goodness of the Lord In the land of the living."

We all want to see God's goodness in our lives. Jesus' half-brother, James, gives us more understanding of God's goodness and blessings toward us. However, it seems there are testing and temptations in our lives too. Look what James has to say on the matter. I believe James knows what he is talking about since he lived and grew up in the same household where Jesus lived.

> *God blesses those who patiently endure testing and temptation. Afterward they will receive the crown of life that God has promised to those who love him. And remember, when you are being tempted, do not say, "God is tempting me." God is never tempted to do wrong, and he never tempts anyone else. Temptation comes from our own desires, which entice us and drag us away. These desires give birth to sinful actions. And when sin is allowed to grow, it gives birth to death.*
>
> *So don't be misled, my dear brothers and sisters. Whatever is good and perfect is a gift coming down to us from God our Father, who created all the lights in the heavens. He never changes or casts a shifting shadow.*
>
> **James 1:12–17 (NLT)**

If you want to experience the goodness of God, you must live according to His ways. Assuming you live to please God, take another look into receiving God's goodness. Listen to what Jesus told the people.

> *Ask, and it will be given to you; seek, and you will find; knock, and it will be opened to you. For everyone who asks receives, and he who seeks finds, and to him who knocks it will be opened. Or what man is there among you who, if his son asks for bread, will give him a stone? Or if he asks for a fish, will he give him a serpent? If you then, being evil, know how to give good gifts to your children, how much more will your Father who is in heaven give good things to those who ask Him!*
>
> **Matthew 7:7–11 (NKJV)**

Sometimes you do not have simply because you did not ask, because you think you are not worthy or good enough to ask God for anything. God's goodness is not about you; it is about God's love for you. You can see by these few verses that you can trust God to be good to you. His goodness toward you never stops, and His goodness toward you never depends on you.

God is holy. You are also holy, not because of anything you have done but because God is holy. However, you are to live a godly life, pleasing God.

Leviticus 19:1–2 (NKJV), "And the Lord spoke to Moses, saying, 'Speak to all the congregation of the children of Israel, and say to them: You shall be holy, for

I the Lord your God am holy.'"

First Peter 1:14–16 (NIV), "As obedient children do not conform to the evil desires you had when you lived in ignorance. But just as he who called you is holy, so be holy in all you do; for it is written: 'Be holy, because I am holy.'"

The Hebrew-Greek Key Study Bible tells us the Hebrew word *Hagios* for *holy* means "separation, consecration, and devotion to the service of God, sharing in God's purity and avoiding the world's defilement" (Zodhiates 1984, 1657).

God considers you holy because He is holy! You cannot make yourself holy. Only God can impart holiness. God set humanity apart to be holy, not animals, plants, flowers, mountains, lakes, seas, moon, stars, or any other object of His creation. He set humanity apart to have a relationship and fellowship with Him for His pleasure, plans, and purposes. The only requirement for being holy is a relationship with Jesus Christ. When you have a relationship with Jesus, your conduct becomes holy as you grow to be more like Him. Your job is to love Jesus and have daily fellowship with Him.

God is faithful. You need to understand that God is always faithful. Being *faithful* means "keeping one's promises." God is always faithful. The Hebrew word for *faithful* is *Pistos,* meaning "certain, worthy to be believed, true, just, and trustworthy" (Zodhiates 1984, #8, 1721).

Now you have every spiritual gift you need as you eagerly wait for the return of our Lord Jesus Christ. He will keep you strong to the end so that you will be free from all blame on the day when our Lord Jesus Christ returns. God will do this, for he is faithful to do what he says, and he has invited you into partnership with his Son, Jesus Christ our Lord.

1 Corinthians 1:7–9 (NLT)

Hebrews 10:23 (NKJV), "Let us hold fast the confession of our hope without wavering, for He who promised is faithful."

The following scriptures tell of His faithfulness but require something from you.

Deuteronomy 7:9 (NKJV), "Therefore know that the Lord your God, He is God, the faithful God who keeps covenant and mercy for a thousand generations with those who love Him and keep His commandments."

First John 1:9 (NKJV), "If we confess our sins, He is faithful and just to forgive us our sins and to cleanse us from all unrighteousness."

These scriptures tell you what God will do for you when you meet His conditions. These are not difficult conditions: *love Him and others, obey Him, and confess your sins*. God keeps His covenant promises for a thousand generations, but only for those who love and follow Him. He is not obligated to keep promises to anyone who rejects Him. However, He is patient and long-suffering, giving many chances to repent and walk with Him.

Everything changes so fast that it's hard to keep up in our world today. But God never changes; however, that is not true of us. With God, His love, goodness, faithfulness, and especially His Word will never change even if we change.

> *So shall My word be that goes forth from My mouth;*
>
> *It shall not return to Me void,*
>
> *But it shall accomplish what I please,*
>
> *And it shall prosper in the thing for which I sent it.*
>
> **Isaiah 55:11 (NKJV)**

Malachi 3:6 (NKJV), "For I am the Lord, I do not change…"

Hebrews 13:8 (NIV), "Jesus Christ is the same yesterday and today and forever."

We have looked at some of God's characteristics; now, let us see some of the attributes He has given to you.

CHAPTER 7:

WHAT CHARACTERISTICS DID GOD GIVE ME?

God has given you some of His characteristics or attributes. The online Merriam-Webster Dictionary defines the word *characteristic* as "a distinguishing trait, quality, or property." For example, God's character is faith, mercy, and grace. Let us see how God's characteristics in you affect you.

Faith. You receive everything from God by faith. But what is faith? Only God can define the kind of faith that pleases Him.

Hebrews 11:1 (TLB), "What is faith? It is the confident assurance that something we want is going to happen. It is the certainty that what we hope for is waiting for us, even though we cannot see it up ahead."

Hebrews 11:6 (TLB), "You can never please God without faith, without depending on Him. Anyone who wants to come to God must believe that there is a God and that He rewards those who sincerely look for Him."

Look at what the apostle Paul said about the measure of faith that God has given you.

Matthew 17:20 (NIV), "He replied, 'Because you have so little faith. Truly I tell you, if you have faith as small as a mustard seed, you can say to this mountain, "Move from here to there," and it will move. Nothing will be impossible for you.'"

Romans 12:3 (NLT), "Because of the privilege and authority God has given me, I give each of you this warning: Don't think you are better than you really are. Be honest in your evaluation of yourselves, measuring yourselves by the faith God has given us."

God has given you the same measure of faith He has given to everyone else. As you study God's Word, your faith will be increased, adding hope to your requests. Hope helps you believe that what you do not see will come to pass. Hope always expects the extraordinary.

Romans 10:17 (NKJV), "So then faith comes by hearing, and hearing by the word of God."

This scripture tells you that your faith can be increased as you read and study the Word of God. If you need wisdom, that comes from God too.

> *If any of you lacks wisdom, let him ask of God, who gives to all liberally and without reproach, and it will be given to him. But let him ask in faith, with no doubting, for he*

> *who doubts is like a wave of the sea driven*
> *and tossed by the wind. For let not that man*
> *suppose that he will receive anything from the*
> *Lord; he is a double-minded man, unstable in*
> *all his ways.*

James 1:5–8 (NKJV)

The words *him* and *he* in the verses in James mean *you*. Therefore, you could put your name in these verses in place of his and not change the context.

Now go to Mark 11:22–25 to understand how to use your faith.

> *Then Jesus said to the disciples, "Have faith*
> *in God. I tell you the truth, you can say to*
> *this mountain, 'May you be lifted up and*
> *thrown into the sea,' and it will happen. But*
> *you must really believe it will happen and*
> *have no doubt in your heart. I tell you, you*
> *can pray for anything, and if you believe that*
> *you've received it, it will be yours. But when*
> *you are praying, first forgive anyone you are*
> *holding a grudge against, so that your Father*
> *in heaven will forgive your sins, too."*

Mark 11:22–25 (NLT)

This Scripture tells you to have faith in God. You may have faith in God, but do you have the God kind of faith shown in Genesis 1:1–26? This portion of Scripture is called "The Six Days of Creation." With everything God created, He spoke it into existence, and then He went to the next day. He did not worry if it had been completed because He expected it to come to pass when He said something. No worries—just expectation! You need to have faith *in* God and the faith *of* God.

Mark also tells you to not allow any doubt when you ask God for something. In Genesis 1: 3-27, God never questioned or wondered whether His creation would happen when He spoke. He wanted to create the earth and all that is in it, so He just said what He wanted to happen, and it happened. The word *said* is the Hebrew word *Amar*, which means "to say, to speak, to declare, to command, and many other words" (Zodhiates 1984, 1579).

When a person commands or declares something, they expect the command to happen. Therefore, no one whispers a declaration; it is spoken with a loud voice.

Through these scriptures in Mark, you can see that you must ask, then believe that you receive, not allowing any doubt about the results of your request; then, you receive by faith. You might wonder, "What can I ask God for?" You can ask for anything He has promised in His written Word. You learn this by studying the Bible. However, it is important to understand that even if the promise is in His Word, sometimes His answer is *yes*, sometimes it is *no,* and sometimes it is to *wait.*

What would happen if you had faith *in* God and the faith *of* God? The faith *of* God means you agree with His Word because His Word becomes your standard for belief and truth. If He said it, it will come to pass unless it is harmful to you or something better is on the horizon. His word never returns void or fails.

The rain and snow come down from the heavens and stay on the ground to water the earth. They cause the grain to grow, producing seed for the farmer and bread for the hungry. It is the same with my word. I send it out, and it always produces fruit. It will accomplish all I want it to, and it will prosper everywhere I send it.

Isaiah 55:10–11 (NLT)

In a ministry meeting I attended, the minister spoke about asking and receiving. Then He said, when you ask, you should say, "Father, in the name of Jesus, I ask for *whatever*. I receive this by faith, and I thank You for it." So when you receive an answer to your prayer request, always thank God for it.

You must have faith to please God. If you cannot please God without faith, you probably need to look closer at faith. *Faith believes in God and His Word.* Faith is not an emotion, a thought, or an experience. Faith is not a formula or recipe that you can work up. Faith comes from knowing that the Word of God is faithful. *Faith is what you believe to be accurate, based on God's written Word so that no one can change your mind.* Faith is also what you believe in the midnight hour of the storm when no one else is around. In those times, do you have hope or despair? Faith turns to God, while anxiety and pain turn to dire circumstances or problems.

When I was diagnosed with breast cancer, doubt came in the darkest hours of the night. I had to fight to keep my faith strong. The devil tried to tell me I would die. But God had told me that I would live and not die. *Remember what you do and what you say determines the outcome.* So I chose to believe God's word to me and not allow doubt to have its victory. God's Word never returns void. But we must accept it, speak it, and praise God for the victory.

> *Do not worry about anything; instead, pray about everything. Tell God what you need, and thank him for all he has done. Then you will experience God's peace, which exceeds anything we can understand. His peace will guard your hearts and minds as you live in Christ Jesus.*

> **Philippians 4:6–7 (NLT)**

Faith does not worry about the situation; instead, faith believes that what God's Word says will turn things around or resolve the problem for your good. When you have faith *in* God and the faith *of* God, you can truthfully say, "God's got this!"

During another very stressful time in my life, I prayed and talked to the Lord about how difficult the problem was. In my heart, I heard, "Where is your faith?" I answered, "I do not have enough faith to do this." I immediately heard, "Will you have enough faith if you add your faith to My faithfulness?" I knew the Lord had spoken to me, and I knew that I would have more than enough faith to walk through the circumstance with His faithfulness. And I did! Faith is not a natural thing, but rather, it is a supernatural gift from God. Faith never requires work, but work always requires faith. *Faith always has power and action.*

God gave you faith to believe in Him and His Word so that you could walk through difficult times. Also, faith is necessary to accomplish the assignments He has given you. You cannot fulfill the plans and purposes God has for you without faith.

Mercy is another characteristic that God has given you. In the online Merriam-Webster Dictionary, *mercy* is defined as "kind or forgiving treatment of someone who could be treated harshly; kindness or help given to people who are in a very bad or desperate situation; compassion showed to an offender or one subject to one's power; lenient treatment; a good or lucky fact or situation."

God not only has mercy, but He *is* mercy. God is love, and He shows His love for you with mercy. *Mercy is God's love in action.* God gives you compassion and pardon when you deserve wrath and punishment. Love and mercy work together and are freely given to you when you are in need. Mercy is God's desire to remove the cause of your distress and the consequences of your sin. His mercy restores you to right standing with Him and cleanses you from any unrighteousness. When God looks at you through His eyes of mercy, He sees you through the blood of Jesus. His mercy overlooks your faults and forgives you when you fail. God is not angry with you.

The Scriptures speak of God's mercy as being forever and available every morning. The Psalms are full of verses telling you about God's mercy.

Psalm 106:1 (NKJV), "Praise the Lord!

"Oh, give thanks to the Lord, for He is good!

"For His mercy endures forever."

Psalm 145:8 (NLT), "The Lord is merciful and compassionate, "slow to get angry and filled with unfailing love."

The prophet Micah gives you another look at the mercy of God.

> *Who is a God like you, who pardons sin and forgives the transgression of the remnant of his inheritance? You do not stay angry forever but delight to show mercy. You will again have compassion on us; you will tread our sins underfoot and hurl all our iniquities into the depths of the sea.*
>
> **Micah 7:18–19 (NIV)**

The apostle Paul gives you another view of God's mercy.

Ephesians 2:4–5 (NLT), "But God is so rich in mercy, and he loved us so much, that even though we were dead because of our sins, he gave us life when he raised Christ from the dead. (It is only by God's grace that you have been saved!)"

The Bible tells you that God's mercy is forever. Many words define His mercy, such as unfailing love, tenderness, kindness, forgiveness, compassion, faithfulness, goodwill, grace, lovingkindness, benevolence, benefit, favor, and more. In addition, the Bible repeatedly mentions that

God's unfailing mercy endures forever.

It is wonderful to know that your merciful Father God loves you so much that He considers each day a fresh, new day with His mercy fresh every morning. He does not remember the sins that He forgave yesterday! God's mercy sees you just as you are, transforming you into the beautiful person He created you.

Geron Davis wrote a beautiful song called "Mercy Saw Me" that talks about how God saw our scars and brokenness through His eyes of mercy. The song's chorus speaks volumes about how God sees you despite your brokenness.

"Beautiful, that's how Mercy saw me, for I was broken and so lost; Mercy looked past all my faults. The justice of God saw what I had done, but Mercy saw me through the Son. Not what I was, but what I could be. That's how Mercy saw me" (Davis 2008).

When babies are born, people say how beautiful they are. They do not say only baby girls are beautiful, but that every baby is beautiful. God does not see you as male or female, instead He sees you as His beautiful child. And mercy sees you blameless, without spot or blemish. Can you see yourself as He sees you—beautiful without a spot or wrinkle?

Grace is another characteristic God has given you. The online Merriam-Webster Dictionary defines *grace* as "unmerited favor or divine assistance; approval, kindness; consideration, thoughtfulness, benevolence, reprieve, exemption."

Before the foundation of the world, God gave grace to all men. Let us see several things about God's grace in and through us.

1. *God's grace is connected to your salvation.*

   Second Timothy 1:9 (NIV), "He has saved us and called us to a holy life—not because of anything we have done but because of his own purpose and grace. This grace was given us in Christ Jesus before the beginning of time."

2. *God's grace is instrumental in your forgiveness.* He forgives you because of the riches of His grace.

   Ephesians 1:7 (NIV), "In him we have redemption through his blood, the forgiveness of sins, in accordance with the riches of God's grace."

   You are saved and forgiven by God's grace, which He freely gives, resulting in absolute pardon by removing all guilt.

3. *Peace is another result of God's grace.*

   Romans 5:1–2 (NKJV), "Therefore, having been justified by faith, we have peace with God through our Lord Jesus Christ, through whom also we have access by faith into this grace in which we stand, and rejoice in hope of the glory of God."

   The words justified by faith are a compound statement with several meanings. The word for *justified* in Greek is dikaiosis, meaning "acquittal, or vindication" (Strong's Concordance #1347, page 143). Therefore, being justified by faith means "God has acquitted or pardoned those whose faith is in Jesus Christ's sacrificial death, burial, and resurrection." By faith in Jesus Christ, a person is freed from guilt and acceptable or righteous in God's eyes.

4. *God's grace redeemed you.*

Romans 3:23–24 (NKJV), "For all have sinned and fall short of the glory of God, being justified freely by His grace through the redemption that is in Christ Jesus."

For the Lord God is a sun and shield;
The Lord will give grace and glory;
No good thing will He withhold
From those who walk uprightly.
Psalm 84:11 (NKJV)

God freely gives you the gift of grace because He loves you. You do not deserve His grace, and you cannot earn it. You can only receive His grace by faith in Jesus' sacrificial death. His supernatural grace is powerful and all-sufficient for every need you have.

I have heard it said that mercy is God not punishing you for what you deserve, and grace is God blessing you even though you do not deserve nor can you earn it. Look what Jesus said to Paul:

Second Corinthians 12:9 (NKJV), "And He said to me, 'My grace is sufficient for you, for My strength is made perfect in weakness.'"

5. *Grace is God's strength for your weakness.*

Hebrews 4:16 (NKJV), "Let us therefore come boldly to the throne of grace, that we may obtain mercy and find grace to help in time of need."

It is comforting to know that His grace gives us strength when we feel weak and are unable to do something. Therefore, His mercy and grace allow us to approach His throne to obtain help when we need it. So the next time you are in trouble or feel weak, boldly approach His throne in prayer and petition, seeking His help with the situation. Because He has given you mercy and grace, you can provide mercy and grace to others.

Before we leave grace, I want to caution you so that you do not misuse God's gift of grace. Many teach that you can live any way you want and expect to receive God's grace. But that is not true. Grace and God's other characteristics in your life are freely given, but obedience is also required. You cannot live a sinful life and expect God's grace.

Forgiveness is another characteristic God has given you. The online Merriam-Webster Dictionary defines *forgiveness* as "absolution, amnesty, pardon, and remission." It is an attitude of your willingness to forgive others.

Psalm 86:5 (NKJV), "For You, Lord, are good, and

ready to forgive,

"abundant in mercy to all those who call upon You."

Psalm 130:4 (NLT), "But you offer forgiveness, that we might learn to fear you."

The Hebrew word *fear* in Psalm 130:4 is *Yârê'*, with two meanings. The first means "to be afraid of something." The second meaning is "a very positive feeling of awe or reverence, which leads to your worship of God" (Zodhiates 1984, 1598).

You can rejoice when you experience forgiveness because you no longer feel guilt or condemnation. You experience peace. In awe of God, you might wonder how He could forgive you. Yet He does! Each time you confess your sins and ask for forgiveness, He forgives you. And He does not remember the transgression or sin. He forgives you for His sake! Isn't that amazing?

First John 1:9 (NLT), "But if we confess our sins to him, he is faithful and just to forgive us our sins and to cleanse us from all wickedness."

According to the online Merriam-Webster Dictionary, *wickedness* in 1 John 1:9 also means "unrighteousness." To be wicked or unrighteous is to have unresolved sin in your life. However, if you repent and ask God for forgiveness, He is quick to forgive you, resulting in you being righteous before God. The word *repent* means "to turn from sin, to feel regret."

Psalm 103:12 (NLT), "He has removed our sins as far from us as the east is from the west."

Isaiah 43:25 (NKJV), "I, even I, am He who blots out your transgressions for My own sake; And I will not remember your sins."

Hebrews 10:17 (NIV), "Then he adds: 'Their sins and lawless acts I will remember no more.'"

> *Who is a God like you,*
> *who pardons sin and forgives the transgression*
> *of the remnant of his inheritance?*
> *You do not stay angry forever*
> *but delight to show mercy.*
>
> **Micah 7:18 (NIV)**

Mark 11:25 (NLT), "But when you are praying, first forgive anyone you are holding a grudge against, so that your Father in heaven will forgive your sins, too."

To understand the impact of God's forgiveness, we need to define several words.

Trespass is defined in the online Merriam-Webster Dictionary as "an unlawful act committed on another person, property, or rights, violating moral or social ethics." A trespass is similar to a transgression.

A *transgression* is "an act against the law, a rule or code of conduct; an offense; cheating or being willingly disobedient." For example, you commit a trespass when you harm another person, their rights, or property. You are committing a transgression when you knowingly run a stop sign, exceed the speed limit, cheat on a test, or tell a lie.

Iniquity is "a deliberate choice without repentance: wickedness and evil actions without remorse."

Sin is "an offense against the religious or moral law, a fault, or a serious shortcoming." For believers, *to sin* means "to miss the mark as an archer misses the target." Sin is doing something opposite from what you know is the right thing to do. God looks at the motives of your heart to determine why you are doing something. You need to ask, "What is the motive of my heart and actions?" For example, "Is my motive to help or hurt someone?"

Sin looks through the motive, ignoring whether your actions are for good or not. Sin can also be an act of omission, meaning not disclosing information that causes hurt or injury to someone. You should ask yourself several other questions to determine your motives:

- What is the motive of your heart when you gossip or lie about others?
- Are you unkind or rude?
- Do you criticize or judge someone just because a person is different from you?
- Are you resentful because you do not get your way?
- How about when you bully someone into getting your way or making others feel inferior to you?

However, if you obey Jesus' commandment to love one another, you will not do things that can hurt others.

John 15:12 (NKJV), "This is My commandment, that you love one another as I have loved you."

All sin separates you from God and the people you love the most. Ultimately, sin causes pain. You will not hurt others if you love someone like Jesus loves you. When teaching or talking with others, I like to ask, "How much has God loved you?" That is how much you must love others. Look at some more scriptures that will remind you how to treat others.

First John 3:18 (NIV), "Dear children, let us not love with words or speech but with actions and in truth."

Galatians 5:26 (NIV), "Let us not become conceited, provoking and envying each other."

Philippians 2:3–4 (NLT), "Don't be selfish; don't try to impress others. Be humble, thinking of others as better than yourselves. Don't look out only for your own interests, but take an interest in others, too."

Take a moment and look at offending others or being offended by someone or something.

Colossians 3:13 (NLT), "Make allowance for each other's faults and forgive anyone who offends you. Remember, the Lord forgave you, so you must forgive others."

The apostle Paul told the Colossians to forgive anyone who offended them. The online Merriam-Webster Dictionary defines the word *offend* as "to cause hurt or pain; to cause difficulty, discomfort, or injury."

In Bible school, I meditated on not being offended for several weeks at the Lord's leading. One day I was in the grocery store deciding what I wanted to serve for a potluck dinner at church. As I stood in the aisle trying to decide what to buy, someone bumped into me and told me to move because I was blocking the aisle. I immediately moved my grocery cart closer to me and apologized for blocking the aisle without looking at the person. Without another thought, I decided what I wanted to purchase, put it in my cart, and moved toward the check-out station as a friend from church stopped me. She said, "I am so sorry for bumping into you and telling you to get out of the aisle. I just saw you, and instead of saying hello, I thought I would tease you a bit. But the Lord told me to come and apologize for what I said to you." We talked for a few minutes, then went our separate ways. I realized that I was not offended at all. Because of her obedience to God's conviction, she was set free from the momentary guilt she felt for being rude to me. Since that time, every time I realize there is an opportunity for me to be offended, I think of that event. If someone hurts you, God will take care of the problem. If you become offended and retaliate, you open yourself up to unforgiveness.

In John Bevere's book *The Bait of Satan*, he addresses the problems of being offended. He tells us that Satan uses a trap to get us into sin. Satan causes us to be offended and uses the offense as bait to draw us into his traps. In today's world, so many people are offended at something or someone, so anger permeates our society. No matter where you turn, you have an opportunity to be offended. Instead of allowing the offense, the apostle Paul told the Ephesians to forgive each other (Bevere 2014).

Ephesians 4:32 (NIV), "Be kind and compassionate to one another, forgiving each other, just as in Christ God forgave you."

When God forgives you, it is as if the offense never happened. He never remembers your mistakes. Forgiving others is sometimes difficult; many times, it hurts too much to let go. You can not or will not forgive because it is human nature to hold onto an offense. But offenses only hurt you; they seldom affect the other person. Unfortunately, the bitterness keeps you from God's best for you.

Stacy Stallings, in her Kindle book *The Easy Way Out*, said, "Forgiveness is more about setting yourself free than setting the other person free" (Stallings 2013).

One of the most difficult things I ever had to forgive was the three men who robbed and murdered my dad. By the time I realized that I had to forgive them, two of the three were dead, but I still had to forgive them. My forgiveness did not make any difference to them, but it set me free. I had to act on my faith that God knew my heart and accepted my heart's desire to obey God and forgive them. Peace comes when you forgive others and yourself, then the offense no longer impacts your day-to-day life. Yes, I miss my dad, but I no longer carry the deep grief I had. You might say you cannot forget what happened, which may be how you feel, but God can help you forgive. It becomes your choice to forgive. You might say, "But you do not know what happened." It makes no difference what happened. Forgiveness sets you free, even if it never affects the other party. While hanging on the cross, Jesus forgave you. He experienced and carried all of your hurts and disappointments for you. You can trust God to help you ignore the offense. Only God's love, mercy, grace, and forgiveness can enable you to forgive and live free from the pain and scars of the past. Only forgiveness can restore His peace and joy in your heart.

I remember reading a story of forgiveness that touched me mightily. Unfortunately, I cannot remember where it was or who wrote it. Nevertheless, I want to share it with you so you can understand how important forgiveness is to God and you.

There was a church in a sizeable north-eastern city that ministered to many types of street people. Many of these people came to the church and were introduced to Jesus. They accepted Him and became strong in their faith and the knowledge of the Lord. One young lady was one of those who accepted Jesus and walked away from her life of sin. Over time, the pastor's son and this young lady fell in love and decided to marry. It was announced to the congregation, which caused an immediate uproar. Many in the church questioned whether it was appropriate for the pastor's son to marry this lady who came from a life of sin. The congregation discussed it over and over again. Finally, the pastor's son stood up and began talking about Jesus, pointing out how Jesus had shed His blood for all sinners. He spoke about how the blood of Jesus washed away all their sin and made them clean and pure in the eyes of God. He reminded them that Jesus had shed His blood for everyone because everyone had sinned and had fallen short of the glory of God, as is mentioned in Romans 3:23. Then, the young man asked them if God had forgiven them. Next, he asked them if the blood of Jesus was still forgiving sinners. Then the pastor's son reminded them that if they still held the young lady's forgiven past against her, then the blood of Jesus could no longer forgive or save anyone. Then he sat down. The pastor's son had reminded them that when they do not forgive others, they negate the blood of Jesus. That precious blood—the very blood of God! We must forgive others and ourselves for holding onto offenses.

I am also reminded of the day I sat in a Bible school class while the instructor taught about forgiveness. He said, "Who are you to remind God of what He has already forgiven and forgotten?" That statement caught my attention! I remembered how often I had held onto something I had already asked God to forgive. I immediately repented and asked the Lord to help me forgive others and myself *completely*. I have since learned that holding onto an offense, even if you have forgiven the person or yourself, is still unforgiveness, and it opens the door for Satan to attack you. Remember there is a God-side and a man-side to everything. God forgives, and you must let go of the offense and hurt.

If you can relate to this, once you have forgiven an offense or hurt, ask God to forgive you for holding onto it. Ask Him to help you let go of any bitterness or resentfulness you might be feeling; then, *you let it go!*

You no longer have to hang on to the torment, misery, and pain of unforgiveness. Torment never comes from God. Whenever you think about why you were holding on to the unforgiveness or offense again, resist the opportunity to rehearse the event, and resist the devil's attempt to bring the event back into your current thinking. Instead, do as James, Jesus' half-brother, tells us to do.

James 4:7 (NKJV), "Therefore submit to God. Resist the devil and he will flee from you."

CHAPTER 8:

HOW DID GOD MAKE ME?

Now that you know who God is and His character, let us see what it means to be made in God's image. To do this, we need to go to Genesis 1:26.

> *Then God said, "Let Us make man in Our image, according to Our likeness; let them have dominion over the fish of the sea, over the birds of the air, and over the cattle, over all the earth and over every creeping thing that creeps on the earth." So God created man in His own image; in the image of God He created him; male and female He created them.*
>
> **Genesis 1:26–27 (NKJV)**

Genesis 1:31 (NKJV), "Then God saw everything that He had made, and indeed it was very good."

Genesis 2:7 (NKJV), "And the Lord God formed man of the dust of the ground, and breathed into his nostrils the breath of life; and man became a living being."

Leviticus 17:11, 14 (NKJV), "For the life of the flesh is in the blood, and I have given it to you upon the altar to make atonement for your souls; for it is the blood that makes atonement for the soul…for it is the life of all flesh. Its blood sustains its life."

God created everything out of nothing except mankind, whom He formed from the dust of the ground. He took something very ordinary—dust and water—then made man in His own image to be extraordinary and unique, just like Himself. Then He breathed life into man. But there is more! God said, "Life is in the blood" (Leviticus 17:14), so He put His blood in us.

I do not know how God put His own blood in us, but I know that we cannot live on earth without blood. I also find it interesting that God designed every part of our physical body to stay in the same place, except for our blood. Our brain, eyes, ears, mouth, nose, feet, legs, arms, hands, bones, muscles, veins, arteries, and organs stay in the exact location and position where God placed them. Yet our blood continually moves throughout our body, bringing life to each part. When blood is restricted in any area, that area stops functioning; it dies.

It is also interesting that regardless of who we are, where we came from, or our skin color, we all have the same red blood flowing through our body, just like Jesus had when He walked as a man on the earth.

The very breath and blood of God gave man life! If

God made humans in His image, what does God look like? Does He have hands and feet, eyes and ears like humans have?

In 2006, Billy Graham answered the question, "Does God have hands and feet and eyes like we do?" His answer was:

> *Even though God is a spiritual being without form or body. He is far greater than any physical being. Sometimes the Bible speaks about God's hands or eyes, but when it does, it is using symbolic language to convey some truth about his activity: "for the eyes of the Lord range throughout the earth to strengthen those whose hearts are fully committed to him" (2 Chronicles 16:9). When the Bible says God created the human race in His image, it means that God put His character or imprint on our souls or spirits. We are not God, but we are like Him (although limited). Because of this, we have the ability to love, and to know right from wrong. Because we bear God's image, we are different from the animals, and all human life is sacred. The tragedy is that God's image within us has been defaced and twisted by sin (although not destroyed). But Christ came to make us whole, and someday "we shall be like him, for we shall see him as he is" (1 John 3:2). In the meantime, make it your goal to grow closer to Christ and serve Him with all of your life.*

> **Graham 2006**

David, the psalmist, was in awe of God. Listen to what he said in Psalm chapter 8.

> *When I consider Your heavens, the work of Your fingers,*
>
> *The moon and the stars, which You have ordained,*
>
> *What is man that You are mindful of him,*
>
> *And the son of man that You visit him?*
>
> *For You have made him a little lower than the angels,*
>
> *And You have crowned him with glory and honor.*
>
> *You have made him to have dominion over the works of Your hands;*
>
> *You have put all things under his feet,*
>
> *All sheep and oxen—*
>
> *Even the beasts of the field,*
>
> *The birds of the air,*
>
> *And the fish of the sea*
>
> *That pass through the paths of the seas.*

Psalm 8:3–8 (NKJV)

King David wrote Psalm chapter 8 when he was a young boy. Can you imagine David as a young shepherd boy sitting in the grass or on a rock watching over his father's sheep? Picture this: It is a quiet night, and all is well. The weather is mild, the moon is shining, and the stars twinkle as he thinks about how awesome and majestic the heavens are. He knows that God is all-powerful. But then, he wonders, "What is man?" Have you ever thought about that? God seems so far away, and we are so small compared to the earth and the universe, so why would God even give us any thought? It never ceases to amaze me that you can see detail on the ground while flying in an airplane at 30,000 feet. Everything is so tiny, but you can still see it. I have thought about how small we must seem to God. And yet, we are so very important to Him! Matthew 10:30 tells us that God knows the number of hairs on our heads. How important is that? We lose hair every day, but God still knows the number of hairs on our heads.

One time, on the way to India to teach in a Bible school, we flew parallel to the Himalayan Mountains when no clouds were surrounding the peaks. They were so beautiful that they almost took my breath away as I wiped away my tears. Even though I knew they were extremely high mountains, they looked small because we were so far from them. Sometimes, that is how we see ourselves, far from God and very small. We ask, just as David, the psalmist, asked, "Who are we, God, that You even consider us?" And, then we change the question, making it personal, and ask, "Who am I, God, that you care about me?"

In *Psalm 8:5*, the word for *angels* is *Eloheim* in Hebrew. If you recall, in Genesis 1:1, we learned that Eloheim is the first covenant name of God. Eloheim includes God the Father, Jesus Christ, His Son, and the Holy Spirit. Therefore, it seems as if we were made just a little lower than God Himself.

Human beings were formed in God's image, while the angels were created. Angels are ministers sent by God for His purposes, but we are the children of God. He made man a bit lower than Himself and gave man dominion over all He had created. Adam even named all the animals, but when Adam disobeyed God and ate the fruit from the forbidden tree, Satan usurped the authority and dominion that God had given to Adam. However, when the time was right, Jesus came and died, taking back that dominion, power, and authority over God's creation. Then He gave us His authority, restoring our dominion over God's creation. Look at what the apostle Paul had to say about angels.

Hebrews 1:14 (NLT), "Therefore, angels are only servants—spirits sent to care for people who will inherit salvation."

Again, in verse 5 of Psalm 8, it also states that not only were we made a little lower than God Himself, but He crowned us with glory and honor. Do you know what that means? The Merriman-Webster Dictionary defines God's *glory* using words such as "brilliance, shining like fire, magnificent, splendid, beautiful, and richly adorned." Richly adorned can represent being embroidered as a tapestry of many colors, each unique. We have different colored hair, eyes, and skin on the outside. Then, we look inside, where our heart is reddish-brown; our lungs and liver are brown. Once again, we look at the colors of our physical bodies. We have white bones, our veins appear blue, and our arteries appear red. And we have the same red blood as Jesus. We shine as a beautifully colored and unique human tapestry, yet our beauty has nothing to do with our efforts. God placed His beauty in and on us!

Ephesians 2:10 (NKJV), "For we are His workmanship, created in Christ Jesus for good works, which God prepared beforehand that we should walk in them."

The word *workmanship*, in Ephesians 2:10, is *poiema*, meaning "manufactured, a product, or a design produced by an artisan" (Hayford 2002, 1647).

The root word for poem and poetry also comes from the Greek word *poiema*. Therefore, we could say that we are God's poetry in motion. Can you imagine yourself as God's work of art? Or see yourself as God's poem of love? That is how God sees you. Can you see yourself as a unique, priceless portrait painted by the God of the universe because of His love for you? No poem or piece of priceless art in any museum can compare to you in God's eyes. Reflect on this and see yourself as He sees you!

David, the shepherd, was also in awe of how God knew and formed him even before he existed.

> *For You formed my inward parts;*
> *You wove me in my mother's womb.*
> *I will give thanks to You, for I am fearfully and wonderfully made;*
> *Wonderful are Your works,*
> *And my soul knows it very well.*

My frame was not hidden from You,

When I was made in secret,

And skillfully wrought in the depths of the earth;

Your eyes have seen my unformed substance;

And in Your book were all written

The days that were ordained for me,

When as yet there was not one of them.

Psalm 139:13–16 (NASB)

God knew His plans for you and how you would respond before the foundation of the earth. He understood you would sometimes fail or reject Him, but you were not a mistake nor a surprise to Him; instead, He has loved you despite your human weaknesses.

So who are you? You are the beautiful child of God that is unlike any other person on earth. He has given you a purpose that only you can fulfill. In His eyes, you are perfect just as you are! If you cannot see yourself as He sees you, ask Him to help you see yourself as He sees you.

Next, you need to understand what it means to be created in God's image. Look what the apostle Paul said to those in the church at Thessalonica.

First Thessalonians 5:23 (NKJV), "Now may the God of peace Himself sanctify you completely, and may your whole spirit, soul, and body be preserved blameless at the coming of our Lord Jesus Christ."

We see the words *spirit*, *soul*, and *body* in 1 Thessalonians

5:23, making you a three-part being like God. Let us look at each part, beginning with your physical body, and see how wonderfully God made you.

YOUR PHYSICAL BODY

On earth, your physical body is your house where you live. It contains and protects all of your bones, organs, and other parts you need for life on earth. Your physical body is the touchable part of your being. It is what the world sees when you walk by. The color of your skin, hair, eyes, height, and weight make you different from others. Your unique physical appearance and differences are how people recognize you. As you grow older, your appearance changes, your body wears out, and eventually, your physical body stops functioning. This *wearing out* is what is known as physical death.

YOUR SOUL

Hebrews 4:12 (NLT), "For the word of God is alive and powerful. It is sharper than the sharpest two-edged sword, cutting between soul and spirit, between joint and marrow. It exposes our innermost thoughts and desires."

According to this scripture, your soul and spirit are not the same, even though many call them the same. Only God's Word gives insight into these two different yet complex parts of your makeup. Your soul is where your character exists, consisting of three parts:

1. Your mind is where you think, learn, and create.

2. Your emotions are how you feel and see things.

3. Your free will gives you the ability to make choices.

Let us learn about the different aspects of your soul, beginning with your mind.

Your mind is the first part of your soul. Your mind is different from your physical brain, making your mind highly complex. It is the seat of your intelligence, thinking, reasoning, understanding, judgment, memory, mental ability, and creativity. As a result, it is different from your feelings, emotional responses, and the choices you might make.

Your mind or intellect allows you to form opinions, develop, and solve problems based on incoming data. You process information using three functions:

1. You obtain knowledge, which is the accumulation of facts, also known as learning.

2. You develop understanding, giving you the ability to put together knowledge and learn to seek direction and solutions.

3. You acquire wisdom, or the ability to interpret and use knowledge.

Proverbs 1:7 (NIV), "The fear of the Lord is the beginning of knowledge..."

Psalm 111:10 (NIV), "The fear of the Lord is the beginning of wisdom;

"all who follow his precepts have good understanding."

Proverbs 9:10 (NIV), "The fear of the Lord is the

beginning of wisdom,

"and knowledge of the Holy One is understanding."

In each of these verses, the word *fear* "does not mean to be afraid of something"; rather, it is *virah* in Hebrew, which means "to be in awe or have respect for someone or something." In these verses, *fear* is "the reverence or awe of God" (Zodhiates 1984, 1598).

When you learn something, you develop knowledge that helps you understand. This combined knowledge and understanding gives you wisdom resulting in solutions. As you learn about God, you are no longer afraid of Him; instead, you develop respect for Him. The more you know Him, the more important your ability for knowledge and understanding becomes. Again, knowledge and experience give you the wisdom that aids in solving questions or problems.

Have you ever watched infants when they discover their hands or feet? First, the infant will watch as their hands or feet move around. Next, the infant grabs and catches their feet, learning how their hands work. Wisdom comes when the infant discovers how to use their hands to grab something on purpose. Next, the infant will develop understanding, allowing them to direct their hands to pick up something they want. Again, watch a puppy as it discovers and chases its tail. The puppy will run in circles until it catches its tail. If the puppy accidentally bites its tail when it catches its tail, the puppy will learn not to bite it because it hurts. That's wisdom!

Understanding is the exercise of the mind to see the entire picture from beginning to end. It looks at how everything fits and works together. Understanding is different from explanation. Understanding considers the whole situation or circumstance, while an explanation or answer sees just what is in front of it.

First Corinthians 2:16 (TLB), "But, strange as it seems, we Christians do have within us a portion of the very thoughts and mind of Christ."

It might be hard to believe, but God's Word tells you that you have the mind of Jesus Christ. When you accept Jesus, the Spirit of Christ, also known as the Holy Spirit, comes to live in you when you are spiritually born again. The Holy Spirit searches the mind of God and tells you what you need to know.

Emotions. The second part of your soul is your emotions, which play a significant role in how you see yourself and others. Many people answer the question of who they are based on outward appearances. How you believe other people see you or feel about you can determine how you feel about yourself. When someone tells you that you will never amount to anything, you stop trying to reach your potential. When someone tells you that you can be anything you want to be, you strive to achieve whatever it is that becomes your passion.

Our society also tells us who we should be, based on how other people think we should look or act. Are you too slim or too fat based on another person's perception? Society tells you what style or color of hair you should have or if your hair is in fashion. Our society also suggests that you need to change to be like everyone else to be accepted. Many magazines, social media, and television advertisements only show young, beautiful people with pleasant lifestyles. When your life does not match that picture, it affects how you see yourself.

These viewpoints only describe how someone else decides who you are or should be, not who you truly are. When you strive to look and act like someone else, your life becomes frustrated. You lose out on who God designed you to be as you try to become someone you are not. Look at some other ways society influences you.

Fashion. Fashion plays an integral part in how you feel about yourself. If you look or dress differently from your peers, you often feel unworthy and left out. This viewpoint tells you to wear socially accepted brands or styles if you want people to accept and welcome you.

I remember being in high school when it was popular for female students to wear very expensive cardigan sweaters with football-shaped buttons. When students could not afford them, they were looked down on and not readily accepted. Today, wearing costly clothing or shoes can still be the benchmark to being taken seriously. Sometimes this can lead to being bullied, causing emotional and physical distress, wounds, and scars. You may think this occurs only with young people, but it happens in every age and gender. When it is impossible to conform to peers due to your circumstances, you may become frustrated, angry, and depressed. You may see yourself as unacceptable, which can even lead to physical death. You feel devalued or marginalized. The Bible tells you not to be overly concerned with your outward appearance but cultivate inward beauty.

First Peter 3:3–4 (NLT), "Don't be concerned about the outward beauty of fancy hairstyles, expensive jewelry, or beautiful clothes. You should clothe yourselves instead with the beauty that comes from within, the unfading beauty of a gentle and quiet spirit, which is so precious to God."

Culture or ancestry. Culture or ancestry can play a significant part in how you see yourself too. Your skin color, religion, and culture suggest who you are, depending on where you live. Again, sometimes people from different cultures see and treat you differently because you do not meet their accepted look or ways. Sometimes, you do the same thing to others. Do you look at a person's heart or their outward appearance?

The Lord looks at a person's heart instead of their outward appearance. Let us look at two events in the Bible that show us how God appoints people for His purposes.

After God renounced King Saul, the first king over the Kingdom of Israel, for disobeying Him, God sent the prophet Samuel to anoint another person to be king. That person was David, the youngest son of Jesse the Bethlehemite, the grandson of Ruth and Boaz. This relationship placed Jesse in the line of God's covenant with Abraham. (Ruth 4:18–21). Therefore any son of Jesse's would be in the line of Abraham too. So, if you continue to read this story, you will see that God anointed David, the youngest son of Jesse, to be the next king over the children of Israel. Let us see what happens when Samuel shows up unexpectantly where Jesse and his sons live.

> *Samuel replied, "Yes, in peace; I have come to sacrifice to the Lord. Consecrate yourselves and come to the sacrifice with me." Then he consecrated Jesse and his sons and invited them to the sacrifice.*
>
> *When they arrived, Samuel saw Eliab and thought, "Surely the Lord's anointed stands here before the Lord."*
>
> *But the Lord said to Samuel, "Do not consider his appearance or his height, for I have rejected him. The Lord does not look at the things people look at. People look at the outward appearance, but the Lord looks at the heart."*
>
> **1 Samuel 16:5–7 (NIV)**

Let us go back to the time of Abraham, his son Jacob, and Jacob's twelve sons. Many years before Samuel anointed Jesse's son David to be king over Israel, Jacob, Abraham's grandson, whose name God had changed to Israel, prophesied over his twelve sons who would become leaders of the nation of Israel (Genesis 49). In that prophecy, Israel prophesied over his fourth son Judah that a king's scepter would never depart from the Kingdom of Judah. At the time of this prophecy, there had never been the Kingdom of Judah and would not be for several hundred years. Let us read the prophecy over Judah.

Genesis 49:10 (NLT), "The scepter will not depart from Judah, nor the ruler's staff from his descendants, until the coming of the one to whom it belongs, the one whom all nations will honor."

Now, let us go back to Samuel. When God rejected King Saul, He set in motion the fulfillment of the prophecy over Judah from years before; Samuel was instructed not to judge a person by their outward appearance.

While working in my financial services business, I talked with an older woman with a heavy foreign accent. I had just met her, so I asked where she was from during our conversation. She did not answer, so I asked again, thinking she had not heard me. Finally, she turned to me with a sad look and said she did not want to tell me because I would not like her. I told her it was more important for me to know her heart than where she was born. Then, she told me she was from a Middle Eastern country. Over time, we became good friends. She was a lovely, intelligent woman that I respected. If I had judged her because she was from a different culture, I would have lost out on a friendship with a wonderful woman.

I also remember going into different cultures as a missionary to Asia. Sometimes, people would treat me differently because of my skin color, language, and clothes because they differed from theirs. Some stores and markets charged more because I was an outsider. Some children who had never seen a person with my hair and skin color would cry or hide in their mother's skirts. I was not readily accepted in their society because I looked different from them.

After being in a village in the Philippines for about two months, I rode on a very crowded bus with my eyes closed, quietly praising the Lord. I felt someone gently touching my knee but ignored it because I thought it was due to the motion of the crowded bus. The pastor traveling with me tapped me on the shoulder and told me to open my eyes. I opened my eyes to see a very small boy, about two years old, patting my knee, saying something in his language that I could not understand. I almost cried when the pastor told me the child was calling me "grandmother" in his native tongue. This toddler was the first child to accept me without crying before he knew me. We all want acceptance regardless of our differences. We must be careful to judge people by their character rather than their looks.

Money is another qualifier. The world says having money proves your worth. People with a lot of money or perceived to have a lot of money are treated differently than people perceived not to have much money. Your character is the true picture and test of your value, not your net worth.

Many years ago, I lived in a town where many millionaire retirees lived. One day, I was at a gas station where a person in work clothes pumped gas for me. He did not look or act like he was wealthy, but I knew him to be very rich. Regardless of his appearance and wealth, he was a humble, retired man who liked to be busy and serve people. I wondered about how he was treated. Did other people treat him kindly? Or did they look at his outward appearance and consider him a person not worthy of respect or kindness? We sometimes judge people by appearance, while God looks at the heart. Regardless of our circumstances, the result of accepting the world's view of who we are is not working. People are discouraged and unhappy. Many people are bullied or abused. What would it be like if everyone was treated the same regardless of their culture, looks, or financial worth? How would we treat others if we could discover who they are and look at the person's heart instead of their circumstances?

The *Daily News* can cause you to be anxious and worry about what is happening around the world. Some reports or comments cause you to judge everything by those reports, whether true or not. Sometimes, the messages are not facts but someone's perception of what is happening. These reports cause fear and unrest in many people.

Today, the obsession with phones and social media is another area that can affect your perception of yourself. Are you on your phone continuously, afraid you will miss something? Do you eat, sleep, work, and play with your phone at your ear? This results in very little interaction between people because there is so much reliance on phones. Texting has taken away the intimate connection of writing a note of thanks, a letter of appreciation, or expressing the love you have for someone you care about.

Do you or someone you know post every detail about your life on social media? Unfortunately, social media messages can lead to gossip that can cause you or others a lot of pain and suffering.

Phones and social media. Many people spend a great deal of time ranting about something or someone, claiming it is their right to their opinion without thinking about how it might hurt another person. However, what you think about and how you respond to these reports can affect how you feel about yourself. The Bible gives you something to consider along this line.

> *Don't worry about anything; instead, pray about everything. Tell God what you need, and thank him for all he has done. Then you will experience God's peace, which exceeds anything we can understand. His peace will guard your hearts and minds as you live in Christ Jesus.*

Philippians 4:6–7 (NLT)

Free will. Our free will is the third part of our soul. The concept of your free will is that God has given you the right and power to exercise your choice without fear. The online Merriam-Webster Dictionary defines *coercion* as "to make someone do something by obligation, force, or threat." Your free will gives you the ability to make choices to determine what you want, what you like, and how to do things without pressure from someone else. As an individual, God gave you the right to make your own choices. Whether a choice is good or bad, it is still your choice. However, every choice has a consequence, and once you have made your choice, you have to accept and deal with the consequences, whether they are right or wrong, good or bad. For instance, you may choose to disobey the law, but if you are arrested, you may have consequences. The same thing happens when you decide to disobey God's Word. He will forgive you, but there may still be consequences.

God's Word also contains many promises that make our lives better. But sometimes, the promises have conditions. Because we have free will, we can accept or reject the promise because of the requirements. One example is God's promise for us to have peace and the conditions to receive the promise. *Peace* means "that you are no longer troubled or worried about the situation." Are you worrying or anxious about something? Let us look at a few scriptures to see how you can have peace instead.

John 14:1 (NLT), "Don't let your hearts be troubled. Trust in God, and trust also in me."

First Peter 5:7 (NIV), "Cast all your anxiety on him because he cares for you."

Romans 5:1 (NLT), "Therefore, since we have been made right in God's sight by faith, we have peace with God because of what Jesus Christ our Lord has done for us."

When you are worried or troubled, you are not peaceful. For the promise of peace, the condition is to trust in God's Son, Jesus Christ, giving Him all of your troubles and cares. You might say, "I do not know how to give my worries and troubles to Jesus." Let us look at an example of how to do this. If I give you my pencil, who will have it? You would, of course! However, if you give the pencil back to me, I will have it again. Is not that correct? When you cast or give your troubles to Jesus, it is the same principle. You give your concerns to Jesus by prayer. In other words, you just talk to Jesus like you are talking to a friend. You ask Jesus to manage the situation. Once you give Him your troubles and requests, He has them and takes on the responsibility to deal with them. If you continue to worry, you take the problem back, and He no longer has control over it. Remember the God-side of your request is for Him to take care of the problem, while the man-side is that you trust Him to do whatever He chooses. Then, you stop worrying about the problem and praise Him for resolving it.

You need to know that His answer might be yes, no, or wait. Wait because it is not the right time. He cares and wants only the best for you. Sometimes, His *no* or *wait* can mean your request might harm you, or something better is going to happen. If you take the anxiety or worry back, then Jesus does not have the problem anymore. You have it again. He will let you manage the situation for as long as you want. Give the problem to Him, and do not take it back. Just be patient and let Him work it out. Whenever you think He has forgotten you, continue to trust and thank Him for your requests. I realize that this is not how the world looks at things, but Jesus is the one that said cast or give all your troubles to Him. You can trust Him, knowing His best is waiting for you just around the corner.

Let us look at a few more promises with their conditions.

Hebrews 11:6 (NIV), "And without faith it is impossible to please God, because anyone who comes to him must believe that he exists and that he rewards those who earnestly seek him."

If you want to please God, you must first believe that God is real. Then, by using your faith, believe that He is willing to reward you when you seek Him. Remember faith is believing and receiving before seeing!

Do you need wisdom?

> *If any of you lacks wisdom, let him ask of God, who gives to all liberally and without reproach, and it will be given to him. But let him ask in faith, with no doubting, for he who doubts is like a wave of the sea driven and tossed by the wind. For let not that man suppose that he will receive anything from the Lord; he is a double-minded man, unstable in all his ways.*
>
> **James 1:5–8 (NKJV)**

This verse tells you how you can receive anything from God. First, in Jesus' name, you ask Father God for whatever you need, and then with faith, you believe that He will give you your request. Then you praise Him for the resolution and answers. James chapter 5 has similar conditions.

Is anyone among you suffering? Let him pray.

Is anyone cheerful? Let him sing psalms. Is anyone among you sick? Let him call for the elders of the church, and let them pray over him, anointing him with oil in the name of the Lord. And the prayer of faith will save the sick, and the Lord will raise him up. And if he has committed sins, he will be forgiven. Confess your trespasses to one another, and pray for one another, that you may be healed. The effective, fervent prayer of a righteous man avails much.

James 5:13–16 (NKJV)

As you read and think about these scriptures, do you see the promises and the conditions? The promises are on God's side—while the conditions are on man's side. *Acknowledging the promises, then meeting the conditions determines the outcome.* The Scriptures give you insight and knowledge about living an abundant life—God's way. The Scriptures also tell you how to treat others. God gave you a free will to choose your path. You may be at a crossroads today. Which way will you go?

YOUR SPIRIT

Finally, let us examine your third part, which is your spirit. As you previously learned, the three parts of your soul consist of:

1. your mind, where you think;
2. your emotions, where you feel; and
3. your free will, where you make choices.

Only God's Word can help you separate and understand the differences between your soul and spirit.

> *For the word of God is living and powerful, and sharper than any two-edged sword, piercing even to the division of soul and spirit, and of joints and marrow, and is a discerner of the thoughts and intents of the heart. And there is no creature hidden from His sight, but all things are naked and open to the eyes of Him to whom we must give account.*
>
> **Hebrews 4:12–13 (NKJV)**

Psalm 119:105 (NKJV), "Your word is a lamp to my feet And a light to my path."

In these scriptures, God's written Word gives understanding to your soul through your mind, your will, and your emotions. His Word illuminates or brings understanding to your thinking, feeling, and decision-making processes. These scriptures speak of God's communication process with your soul through His Word.

God's written Word →

directs your feet or path to action →

to bring understanding to your plans →

to ensure your success.

Your spirit is who you are and serves another purpose. For example, when God formed Adam, who represented all human beings, He breathed His very life into him, causing Adam to be a living being.

Genesis 2:7 (NKJV), "And the Lord God formed man

of the dust of the ground, and breathed into his nostrils the breath of life; and man became a living being."

When God breathed into Adam, He not only made Adam a living being, but Adam became an eternal spirit being like God Himself.

First Corinthians 2:11 (NKJV), "For what man knows the things of a man except the spirit of the man which is in him? Even so no one knows the things of God except the Spirit of God."

The *spirit of man*, which separates man from animals, is where God communicates with you, sharing His true nature. It is where God, the Holy Spirit, teaches, corrects, directs, and reminds you of His Word.

Proverbs 20:27 (NKJV), "The spirit of a man is the lamp of the Lord, Searching all the inner depths of his heart."

You could turn this scripture around to read, "The lamp of the Lord searches the spirit of man to determine man's motives." Let us read the same Scripture in The Living Bible.

Proverbs 20:27 (TLB), "A man's conscience is the Lord's searchlight exposing his hidden motives."

God placed a conscience in you, that small still voice in your innermost being, which exposes your motives. Your conscience is God's way of helping you know the difference between good and evil.

The Bible calls your redeemed spirit, the innermost part of you, the temple of the Holy Spirit.

First Corinthians 3:16 (NKJV), "Do you not know that you are the temple of God and that the Spirit of God dwells in you?"

The word *temple* in Hebrew means "the habitation of God." Therefore, it is interesting that the Old Testament high priest was permitted to enter the holy of holies once a year on the Day of Atonement for himself and the people.

Hebrews 9:7 (NLT), "But only the high priest ever entered the Most Holy Place, and only once a year. And he always offered blood for his own sins and for the sins the people had committed in ignorance."

But Jesus changed all of that for you. He calls you a royal priesthood, giving you access to the heavenly holy of holies anytime you desire to praise and worship Him.

First Peter 2:9 (NKJV), "But you are a chosen generation, a royal priesthood, a holy nation, His own special people, that you may proclaim the praises of Him who called you out of darkness into His marvelous light."

God had His dwelling place in the Old Testament tabernacle and temple, but now because of Jesus' death, burial, and resurrection, He has chosen to live in born-again believers. God considers your redeemed spirit as the dwelling place for His Holy Spirit. He called you a chosen generation, a royal priesthood, a holy nation, and His very own special people.

To summarize, your spirit is your true inner person where God communicates with you and where the Holy Spirit, the Spirit of Christ, lives in you.

CHAPTER 9:

WHAT ARE GOD'S GIFTS TO ME?

God made us a beautiful work of art, and He placed some of His characteristics in us and made us the temple or dwelling place of the Holy Spirit. However, God also gave us gifts that make us even more unique and special. There are three distinct sets of gifts mentioned in the Bible.

1. The ministry gifts Jesus gave to the church:

    And He Himself gave some to be apostles, some prophets, some evangelists, and some pastors and teachers, for the equipping of the saints for the work of ministry, for the edifying of the body of Christ, till we all come to the unity of the faith and of the knowledge of the Son of God, to a perfect man, to the measure of the stature of the fullness of Christ.

    Ephesians 4:11–13 (NKJV)

2. The gifts the Holy Spirit gave to each believer in Jesus Christ:

    There are diversities of gifts, but the same Spirit. There are differences of ministries, but the same Lord. And there are diversities of activities, but it is the same God who works all in all. But the manifestation of the Spirit is given to each one for the profit of all: for to one is given the word of wisdom through the Spirit, to another the word of knowledge through the same Spirit, to another faith by the same Spirit, to another gifts of healings by the same Spirit, to another the working of miracles, to another prophecy, to another discerning of spirits, to another different kinds of tongues, to another the interpretation of tongues. But one and the same Spirit works all these things, distributing to each one individually as He wills.

    First Corinthians 12:4–11 (NKJV)

3. The gifts Father God gave to each person:

    Having then gifts differing according to the grace that is given to us, let us use them: if prophecy, let us prophesy in proportion to our faith; or ministry, let us use it in our ministering; he who teaches, in teaching; he who exhorts, in exhortation; he who gives, with liberality; he who leads, with diligence; he who shows mercy, with cheerfulness.

    Romans 12:6–8 (NKJV)

Don and Katie Fortune wrote a book called *Discover*

Your God-Given Gifts (Fortune 1987). All my life, I knew I was different but never knew why until I learned about the gifts Father God gave me. As I read and studied these gifts, I realized why I was different and how special I am to God and His plans for me. When God breathed life into each of us, He gifted us with spiritual gifts. You have been given these gifts too. As you learn more about yourself and these gifts, you will see another part of the real you. You will see how special God made you. There is no one just like you in God's eyes.

This chapter will look only at the seven gifts the Father has given us, detailed in Romans 12:6–8. These gifts are practical gifts that motivate us to accomplish His plans and purposes for our life, and they also shape our personality and character.

As we look briefly at the gifts, we will use the name of each gift by its function rather than by its office. For example, the office of the prophet is to foretell the plans and purposes of God. The gift is not the office of the prophet but the prophet's function to perceive and understand the will of God in a specific situation. Therefore, we will use the term "perceiver" instead of "prophet" to avoid confusion with the office. Also, for clarification purposes, we will use the gift of compassion instead of the gift of mercy.

We will look at the function and how the gift meets spiritual needs in the body of Christ. Finally, we will identify a couple of people in the Bible who demonstrate the gift in their life.

1. The perceiver is a person who clearly receives or perceives the will and purpose of God. The perceiver likes to disciple, intercede, enforce, admonish, and dramatize God's words. This gift meets spiritual needs by keeping us centered on spiritual principles and represents the eyes of the body. Jeremiah and John the Baptist are examples of perceivers.

2. The server loves to serve others by meeting practical needs. The server likes to assist, build, fix, and follow rather than lead, produce, or maintain. This gift keeps the work of the ministry moving forward and represents the hands of the body. Martha and Stephen are examples of servers.

3. The teacher loves to research and communicate truth. The teacher likes to analyze and solve problems, discover, educate, research, and communicate. This gift meets mental needs and keeps us studying and learning God's Word. It represents the mind of the body. Timothy and Luke are examples of teachers.

4. The exhorter encourages personal growth and progress. The exhorter likes to coach, motivate, inspire, counsel, and advocate. This gift meets psychological needs and keeps us applying spiritual truths in our actions and behavior. It represents the mouth of the body. Aaron and Barnabas are examples of exhorters.

5. The giver shares material assistance and support. The giver likes to give, assist, help, support, witness, and evangelize. This gift meets material

needs and keeps us sharing and providing for specific needs. It represents the arms of the body. Abraham and Cornelius are examples of givers.

6. The administrator gives leadership and direction. The administrator likes to pioneer, envision, oversee, develop, motivate, and achieve. This gift keeps us organized and increases our vision. It represents the shoulders of the body. Joseph and Nehemiah are examples of administrators.

7. The gift of compassion provides personal and emotional support. The compassionate person likes to comfort, rescue, restore, affirm, and nurture and is a crusader who meets our emotional needs, keeping us in the right attitude. This gift represents the heart of the body. The good Samaritan and Ruth are examples of compassionate people.

Don and Katie discovered that some gifts occur more frequently than others, yet no gift has greater value or importance over another. They found on average, perceivers occur 12 percent of the time, servers occur 17 percent of the time, teachers occur 6 percent time, exhorters occur 16 percent of the time, givers occur 6 percent of the time, administrators occur 13 percent of the time, and the compassionate gift occurs 30 percent of the time (Fortune 1987, 26).

The Father gives you the gifts to equip you for the assignments He gives you as you understand and minister to others. You have some characteristics from all of the gifts, but usually, you will only have one or two primary gifts. Identifying your gifts will help you understand who you are, enabling you to cooperate with God's plan.

If you choose to read and study Don and Katie's book *Discover Your God-Given Gifts*, use the questions on the profile pages to determine your giftings. Remember no gift is greater than any other. Be honest with yourself and do not try to make yourself be something you are not. God requires all the gifts to be in operation to accomplish His plans. Therefore, He has gifted you to meet His special purposes for your life. No one else is exactly like you. My prayer for you is that you discover who you are and that your life will take on a new purpose and meaning.

Now, let us see how God's Word will help you prepare to fulfill your God-given purpose. These words have been spoken to many people in the past, but today, they are speaking directly to you.

Psalm 139:16 (NLT), "You saw me before I was born. Every day of my life was recorded in your book. Every moment was laid out before a single day had passed."

Jeremiah 29:11–13 (NLT), "'For I know the plans I have for you,' says the Lord. 'They are plans for good and not for disaster, to give you a future and a hope. In those days when you pray, I will listen. If you look for me wholeheartedly, you will find me.'"

Psalm 32:8–9 (NIV), "I will instruct you and teach you in the way you should go; I will counsel you with my loving eye on you. Do not be like the horse or the mule, which have no understanding but must be controlled by bit and bridle or they will not come to you."

Philippians 2:13 (NLT), "For God is working in you, giving you the desire and the power to do what pleases him."

Nothing you do is a surprise to God. He gifted you to accomplish His purposes and recorded every part of your life in the Book of Life (Luke 10:20, Philippians 4:3). He will bless you beyond your wildest dreams when you choose to follow Him. But if you choose to ignore or disobey Him, you might find life difficult.

Philippians 1:6 (NLT), "And I am certain that God, who began the good work within you, will continue his work until it is finally finished on the day when Christ Jesus returns."

Ephesians 3:20 (NLT), "Now all glory to God, who is able, through his mighty power at work within us, to accomplish infinitely more than we might ask or think."

First Thessalonians 5:23–24 (NLT), "Now may the God of peace make you holy in every way, and may your whole spirit and soul and body be kept blameless until our Lord Jesus Christ comes again. God will make this happen, for he who calls you is faithful."

Knowing your giftings will help you cooperate with God's plan for your life. No one else can fill your place. You were uniquely made, gifted, and equipped to accomplish God's special purposes for your life.

Someone said, "What you are is God's gift to you, and what you make of yourself is your gift to God!" I believe this to be a true statement. When you know how God gifted you, using those gifts brings glory to God.

CHAPTER 10:
WHY IS MY LIFE SUCH A MESS?

"If God loves me so much and made me so wonderful, why is my life such a mess? Is there any hope for me?" The partial answer to this age-old question is in the book of Genesis.

> *Then God said, "Let Us make man in Our image, according to Our likeness; and let them rule over the fish of the sea and over the birds of the sky and over the cattle and over all the earth, and over every creeping thing that creeps on the earth." God created man in His own image, in the image of God He created him; male and female He created them.*
>
> **Genesis 1:26–27 (NASB)**

> *Then the Lord God took the man and put him into the garden of Eden to cultivate it and*

> keep it. The Lord God commanded the man,
> saying, "From any tree of the garden you may
> eat freely; but from the tree of the knowledge
> of good and evil you shall not eat, for in the
> day that you eat from it you will surely die."
> **Genesis 2:15–17 (NASB)**

Genesis 2:18 (NASB), "Then the Lord God said, 'It is not good for the man to be alone; I will make him a helper suitable for him.'"

God made Adam in His image, but Adam was not God. The Bible says the earth and everything in it are owned and belong to God.

Psalm 24:1 (NIV), "The earth is the Lord's, and everything in it, the world, and all who live in it."

As the owner of the earth and everything in it, God gave Adam the task of subduing the garden and having dominion over all creation. However, Adam was not the owner of the earth but was to be the caretaker of God's property. So we need to define several words to understand how this affects you.

The online Merriam-Webster Dictionary Dictionary defines *subdue* as "to conquer or bring under control; to cultivate."

The Hebrew-Greek Study Bible defines *dominion* as "the supreme authority and having absolute ownership." These are terms used in the practice of law. The Hebrew word is *Râdâh*, #7287, meaning "to subdue, have dominion, and reign over" (Zodhiates 1984, 1637).

Adam was to "tend or farm" the land in God's garden. A farmer prepares or cultivates the ground for planting, plants the seeds and plants, then tends the plants by watching over them until they are ready for harvest. God gave the task of caring for the garden to Adam, who was the prototype for all humanity. Man was and is God's crowning achievement in creation! God created and formed Adam to take care of His creation in every way. With authority and a God-given right, Adam named all the animals, fish, and birds. The earth and all that is in it belong to God, but Adam was to watch over God's creation. As with everything owned by someone else, there were rules and procedures to follow. Before He fashioned Eve, God told Adam he could eat the fruit of every tree in the garden except the tree of the knowledge of good and evil. Adam already understood the concept of good. However, eating the fruit of this specific tree gave Adam and Eve an understanding of evil too.

In the process of Adam naming the animals, there was nothing found that was suitable to be his helpmate. Therefore, God decided Adam needed someone to help him, so He formed Eve from Adam's ribs. They enjoyed an intimate relationship with God and each other as they went about their daily routine in the garden.

> *He gave names to all the livestock, all the birds of the sky, and all the wild animals. But still there was no helper just right for him. So the Lord God caused the man to fall into a deep sleep. While the man slept, the Lord God took out one of the man's ribs and closed*

up the opening. Then the Lord God made a woman from the rib, and he brought her to the man.

"At last!" the man exclaimed.

"This one is bone from my bone,

and flesh from my flesh!

She will be called 'woman,'

because she was taken from 'man.'"

Genesis 2:20–23 (NLT)

Sometime later, a serpent entered the garden and began a dialogue with Eve, telling her how good the fruit was on the forbidden tree—the tree of the knowledge of good and evil.

Now the serpent was more crafty than any beast of the field which the Lord God had made. And he said to the woman, "Indeed, has God said, 'You shall not eat from any tree of the garden'?" The woman said to the serpent, "From the fruit of the trees of the garden we may eat; but from the fruit of the tree which is in the middle of the garden, God has said, 'You shall not eat from it or touch it, or you will die.'" The serpent said to the woman, "You surely will not die! For God knows that in the day you eat from it your eyes will be opened, and you will be like God, knowing good and evil." When the woman saw that the tree was good for food, and that it was a delight to the eyes, and that the tree was desirable to make one wise, she

*took from its fruit and ate; and she gave also
to her husband with her, and he ate. Then the
eyes of both of them were opened, and they
knew that they were naked; and they sewed
fig leaves together and made themselves loin
coverings.*

Genesis 3:1–7 (NASB)

To understand why this is important, you need to identify the serpent.

Revelation 12:9 (NLT), "This great dragon—the ancient serpent called the devil, or Satan, the one deceiving the whole world—was thrown down to the earth with all his angels."

The devil, also known as Satan, is an evil spirit who slanders, falsely accuses, and divides without cause. First, he attacks you when you are most vulnerable, then He deceives and pushes you into actions that you know are inappropriate or not good for you. Then, he accuses you of the very act you committed, resulting in your feelings of guilt. He is your adversary and opponent. He also slanders and blasphemes God.

In Hebrew, *Sâṭan*, #7853, means "to attack, oppose, accuse, be an adversary, an accuser, slanderer, seducer, and a *liar*" (Zodhiates 1984, 1645).

He likes to cause division and friction between two or more people. Satan's nature is to attack, kill, and destroy everything good. Whenever He can, Satan will attack your body with diseases, your mind with doubt and perversion, and your relationships with God and others. If that is not enough, he will strike your livelihood, wealth, and reputation. Jesus, speaking to the Pharisees, defined Satan, also called the devil, as a murderer and a liar.

John 8:44 (NIV), "You belong to your father, the devil, and you want to carry out your father's desires. He was a murderer from the beginning, not holding to the truth, for there is no truth in him. When he lies, he speaks his native language, for he is a liar and the father of lies."

Let us go back to the garden. The serpent deceived Eve by convincing her that it was all right to ignore God's command not to eat the fruit from the tree. He also convinced Eve that God was a liar and they would not die if they ate the fruit. Finally, taking the form of a serpent, Satan seduced Eve and convinced her that the fruit would taste wonderful. It is interesting how seduction seems pleasant, but it often brings heartbreak.

Genesis 3:6 (NIV), "When the woman saw that the fruit of the tree was good for food and pleasing to the eye, and also desirable for gaining wisdom, she took some and ate it. She also gave some to her husband, who was with her, and he ate it."

When Adam willingly ate the fruit, he chose to disobey God, bringing sin into his life. Satan rejoices because he knows that sin pleases you for a time but causes separation, pain, and guilt. His job is to stop God's plans through you and for you. But you can resist Him!

> *So humble yourselves before God. Resist the devil, and he will flee from you. Come close*

to God, and God will come close to you. Wash
your hands, sinners; purify your hearts, for
your loyalty is divided between God and the
world. Humble yourselves before the Lord,
and he will lift you up in honor.

James 4:7–8, 10 (NLT)

If you continue to read the story in Genesis, you will find that God removed Adam and Eve from the garden to protect them. However, they did not die a physical death for many years. Instead, they experienced spiritual death, which is separation from God. Their life of relative ease became one of toil, hardship, and distress. God was not angry with them; rather, He loved them enough to protect them from the knowledge and results of evil. But their sin separated them from God and the close relationship they had with Him. Today, God speaks to you through His Word to protect you from circumstances that cause pain, guilt, and separation from Him.

Romans 6:23 (NLT), "For the wages of sin is death, but the free gift of God is eternal life through Christ Jesus our Lord."

Death always separates. For instance, physical death results in separation when a loved one dies. Emotional death occurs when your actions separate you from those you love, such as divorce or estrangement. Finally, spiritual death separates you from God.

Genesis 3:7 (NIV), "Then the eyes of both of them were opened, and they realized they were naked; so they sewed fig leaves together and made coverings for themselves."

Sin stripped Adam and Eve of their innocence. They felt exposed, naked, and guilty, so they tried to fix the problem by sewing fig leaves together to cover themselves. But unfortunately, the leaves could not correct their sin and guilt problems.

Genesis 3:21 (NLT), "And the Lord God made clothing from animal skins for Adam and his wife."

God saw their condition and took pity on them in His great mercy. Even after they disobeyed, God's mercy loved them enough to cover their nakedness with the skins of an innocent animal whose shed blood covered their sins.

Genesis 3:22 (NLT), "Then the Lord God said, 'Look, the human beings have become like us, knowing both good and evil. What if they reach out, take fruit from the tree of life, and eat it? Then they will live forever!'"

God knew if the man stayed in the garden and ate of the tree of life, there would be no hope for him. Satan had stolen Adam's place of authority and power. Now, man would know the difference between good and evil, and he would have no ability to change the circumstances. Humanity was without hope. Sin always has consequences.

Adam and Eve's sin passed to you and everyone who has lived—past, present, and future. What a sad situation! Only God can fix the sin issue! In Genesis 3, God began His plan to redeem all of humanity. He established a sacrifice of innocent blood to cover the sin—the blood of the innocent for the guilty. Remember life is in the blood.

It had to be the offering of innocent blood to redeem and restore guilty humanity to fellowship with God.

When God killed the innocent animals to fashion the garments for Adam and Eve, God's judgment upon the sinless animals provided a covering for the guilty. That was good for Adam and Eve, but how is my mess resolved? Is there any hope for me?

Earlier, we saw that the problem was partly due to Adam and Eve's disobedience. The rest of the problem is we are all descendants of Adam with the same rebellious, sinful nature. We make decisions without God's guidance; instead, we do what we want to do when we want to do it. The world tells us in words and pictures what we should do; everything is designed to make us feel good, look good, and partake of pleasure without regard for God or others. We seldom think about how our actions affect others because everything is for our benefit. By living this way, you receive worldly blessings that fade away. But God says, "Give!" You need to give your time, talent, and resources to others if you want God's gifts of provision, peace, joy, and comfort.

Luke 6:38 (NIV), "Give, and it will be given to you. A good measure, pressed down, shaken together and running over, will be poured into your lap. For with the measure you use, it will be measured to you."

When you become a giver, God promises you blessings based on your generosity. First, however, you must listen to the Holy Spirit, especially in your financial giving. I want to tell you several stories to explain why it is important for you to listen to the Holy Spirit when giving monetary gifts. While visiting another missionary friend in Asia, we went shopping. I was fairly new on the mission field, so my friend taught me to be observant and listen to the Holy Spirit, especially in giving money. To illustrate this, my friend pointed to a woman wearing a very dirty, torn dress with an unkempt baby on her hip. The woman was approaching others for money, which she probably needed, but the reality was the money she collected was not for her or her baby. As the woman asked for money, she frequently looked over her shoulder where her handler was watching. My friend knew this because she had approached the same woman several days before and asked the baby's name. The woman looked at the same person who was watching her. The woman ignored the question and walked away. My friend knew it was common practice to borrow a child to play on the emotions of others and get more money for the handler; any money would not benefit the woman and the baby. The lesson was that God gives us the provision to accomplish His assignments, so we must learn to be good stewards. I am not saying you should not give, but first, listen to the Holy Spirit. God has given you provision not only for yourself but also to accomplish the assignments He has given you.

The same thing happens with beggar children in many parts of the world. The money they collect goes to someone not interested in their welfare. To illustrate this, let me explain. Another time, I was with a group of students and teachers from a Bible school on an evening picnic in a park. Children were hanging around asking for money. Instead, we offered them food, but most of the children left without accepting the food. If they had accepted our offer of food, their handlers, who were watching, would mistreat them; therefore, they refused to accept food even if they were hungry. Satan will play on your emotions with the effect of stealing your money and provision without helping others. It would be helpful for you to become aware that not everything is as it seems.

Another time, I was in a kingdom in Asia. A man dressed as a beggar with only one leg was sitting on the steps of a temple, asking for money. Later, the local pastor told us the man was one of the richest men in the area. Once again, this would have been a misuse of God's money.

If you want God's blessing, it is important to listen to the leading of the Holy Spirit, not only in giving money but in your time and talent as well. Your provision belongs to God, and He wants you to be a giver, so learn to listen to Him, then watch Him give you blessings beyond your expectations.

Haggai 2:8 (NIV), "'The silver is mine and the gold is mine,' declares the Lord Almighty."

I mention these events because listening to the Holy Spirit is always important, especially when giving gifts. The Bible tells you that silver and gold belong to God. Therefore, you must be good stewards if you want the blessings from giving.

Your life might be messed up because it is human

nature to rebel against authority, especially God and His Word. God gave every man free will, meaning you can choose right or wrong, good or evil, just as Adam and Eve did. You can choose to obey God's Word and His directions for you or ignore God and follow your path. Unfortunately, your life is often messy because of your rebellious heart and sinful nature. Obeying God and His Word is your solution to the chaos caused by rebellion and disobedience. Jesus said He came so that we could have an abundant life. If you have been rebellious toward God, repent and ask Him to forgive you.

If your life is a mess, take time to seek God's will for your life as you examine your thoughts, finances, and motives. God wants you to be free from the bondage of the world's ways and the mess in your life.

CHAPTER 11:
IS THERE ANY HOPE FOR ME?

Yes, there is hope for you!

John 10:10 (NKJV), "The thief does not come except to steal, and to kill, and to destroy. I have come that they may have life, and that they may have it more abundantly."

Isaiah 59:16 (NLT), "He was amazed to see that no one intervened to help the oppressed. So he himself stepped in to save them with his strong arm, and his justice sustained him."

Psalm 68:20 (NLT), "Our God is a God who saves! The Sovereign Lord rescues us from death."

Many people feel hopeless when it comes to their life, but Jesus came to save us. So, let us look at the events of Jesus' birth to find hope.

> *This is how Jesus the Messiah was born. His mother, Mary, was engaged to be married to Joseph. But before the marriage took place, while she was still a virgin, she became*

pregnant through the power of the Holy Spirit. Joseph, to whom she was engaged, was a righteous man and did not want to disgrace her publicly, so he decided to break the engagement quietly.

As he considered this, an angel of the Lord appeared to him in a dream. "Joseph, son of David," the angel said, "do not be afraid to take Mary as your wife. For the child within her was conceived by the Holy Spirit. And she will have a son, and you are to name him Jesus, for he will save his people from their sins." All of this occurred to fulfill the Lord's message through his prophet: "Look! The virgin will conceive a child! She will give birth to a son, and they will call him Immanuel, which means 'God is with us.'" When Joseph woke up, he did as the angel of the Lord commanded and took Mary as his wife. But he did not have sexual relations with her until her son was born. And Joseph named him Jesus.

Matthew 1:18–25 (NLT)

In their culture, the marriage commitment was a two-part ceremony like ours. The first part was an engagement ceremony, which took place as they exchanged a robe, coat, or another garment, signifying that the commitment was binding and unbreakable. Only divorce or death could break the engagement commitment. After the ceremony, the groom-to-be would leave to prepare their home.

The second part would happen when the bridegroom's

father pronounced their home finished. The bridegroom would then come for his bride, and they would have the marriage celebration and supper. He would then take his bride to their home. If either party died before the actual marriage, the survivor would be considered a widow or widower. If either party was unfaithful, it was considered an act of adultery, and a divorce would occur. Stoning was the punishment for a woman thought to be unfaithful.

When Mary became pregnant, but not with his child, Joseph did not want Mary to be treated badly or stoned, so he decided to divorce her quietly.

During the night, in a dream, the angel of the Lord told Joseph that the child was the Son of God and to take Mary as his wife. Joseph, a man of faith, believed and obeyed the angel of the Lord and accepted Mary as His wife. God chose Joseph, a righteous man, to care for and protect Jesus and Mary even though Jesus was not his biological child.

It seemed to Joseph that Mary had been unfaithful in the natural, but God told him that Mary had not been unfaithful in a dream. So, as Joseph was a godly man, he chose to listen to God and take Mary as his wife. Knowing and listening to God is important even when it seems to go against everything you see or understand. So let us go back to Mary and Joseph's story.

> At that time the Roman emperor, Augustus, decreed that a census should be taken throughout the Roman Empire. (This was the first census taken when Quirinius was

> *governor of Syria.) All returned to their own*
> *ancestral towns to register for this census.*
> *And because Joseph was a descendant of*
> *King David, he had to go to Bethlehem in*
> *Judea, David's ancient home. He traveled*
> *there from the village of Nazareth in Galilee.*
> *He took with him Mary, to whom he was*
> *engaged, who was now expecting a child.*
>
> **Luke 2:1–5 (NLT)**

The current emperor or king, Caesar Augustus, decided to conduct a census to count the people. Both Joseph and Mary were descendants of King David, requiring them to travel to Bethlehem to be registered in the census. Joseph, the legal guardian for the unborn Jesus, was a descendant of King David, making Jesus a legal heir to the throne. In addition, Jesus' mother, Mary, was also an heir to the throne of David through the line of David's son Nathan, the third son of King David and Bathsheba. Jewish genealogies did not include women, so Mary's lineage is briefly mentioned through the line of Nathan (Luke 3:23, 31). Therefore, with both Joseph and Mary heirs to the throne of David, Jesus was legally and naturally an heir to the throne.

There were no rooms available when they reached Bethlehem due to the large crowds coming to register. So they used space in a stable where Jesus, the Son of God, was laid in a manger after he was born. What a time it was! Even though we sing "Silent Night," it was not silent at all! Heaven rejoiced over His birth as the host of angels sang in praise and worship. Shepherds, who heard the angels singing, came in awe to visit the newborn baby! And, later even the wise men, who most likely came from Persia, sought Him out, bringing Him royal gifts.

Some people say Jesus was only a man, perhaps even a good man and a good teacher, which is true, but it is still not the whole story. True, Jesus was all man because He was born as a human baby, but He was and still is fully God—part of the Trinity: God the Father; Jesus, the Son; and the Holy Spirit.

The apostle John gives us more insight into who this baby Jesus is and the hope He brings you.

John 1:1–4 (NIV), "In the beginning was the Word, and the Word was with God, and the Word was God. He was with God in the beginning. Through him all things were made; without him nothing was made that has been made. In him was life, and that life was the light of all mankind."

John 1:14 (NIV), "The Word became flesh and made his dwelling among us. We have seen his glory, the glory of the one and only Son, who came from the Father, full of grace and truth."

According to the apostle John and ancient history, we know that Jesus was born and lived on the earth. So why did Jesus come to earth as a man? The answer is God loves us! Because of Adam and Eve's disobedience, we were a hopeless people, but when Jesus was born, He brought hope to the world. He was the Redeemer whom God had promised Adam and Eve would come to their rescue (Josephus 1998, 18.3.3, 20.9.1).

John 3:16–17 (NASB), "For God so loved the world, that He gave His only begotten Son, that whoever believes in Him shall not perish, but have eternal life. For God did not send the Son into the world to judge the world, but that the world might be saved through Him."

To answer your question, "Is there any hope for me?" Yes, there is hope for you! But first, you must see yourself as the person God loves and has redeemed. If you had been the only one, He would have still died for you. He still would have paid the sin debt you owed with His death.

The problem is that people cannot pay the price owed for their sin; they can only receive the gift of forgiveness and redemption when they accept Jesus' sacrifice. Are you willing to accept His sacrifice? If you are, you can have hope that Father God will claim you as His beloved child. When you accept Jesus, you become a member of the family of God! An heir to the promises of the covenant.

Ephesians 1:7–8 (NIV), "In him we have redemption through his blood, the forgiveness of sins, in accordance with the riches of God's grace that he lavished on us. With all wisdom and understanding."

Romans 8:16–17 (NASB), "The Spirit Himself testifies with our spirit that we are children of God, and if children, heirs also, heirs of God and fellow heirs with Christ, if indeed we suffer with Him so that we may also be glorified with Him."

> *But when the fullness of the time came, God*
> *sent forth His Son, born of a woman, born*

under the Law, so that He might redeem those who were under the Law, that we might receive the adoption as sons. Because you are sons, God has sent forth the Spirit of His Son into our hearts, crying, "Abba! Father!" Therefore you are no longer a slave, but a son; and if a son, then an heir through God.

Galatians 4:4–7 (NASB)

For you are all sons...of God through faith in Christ Jesus. For all of you who were baptized into Christ have clothed yourselves with Christ. There is neither Jew nor Greek, there is neither slave nor free man, there is neither male nor female; for you are all one in Christ Jesus. And if you belong to Christ, then you are Abraham's descendants, heirs according to promise.

Galatians 3:26–29 (NASB)

Yes, there is hope for you because of God's plan of redemption. Let us find out what that plan is and how it brings hope to you and the many other hopeless people in the world.

CHAPTER 12:

WHAT IS GOD'S PLAN OF REDEMPTION?

Let us fast forward from Jesus' birth to His death. He taught, preached, healed the sick, and delivered the oppressed and hopeless for over three years. When He was about thirty-three and one-half years old, He willingly died on the cross of Calvary to pay for your sins, redeem you to the Father, and forgive you as well. So we are not without hope; we have hope because of God's plan of redemption.

Let us look at an example of hopelessness in John 4:3–15 to see how it affects you. This is the story of the Samaritan woman at a well. In the middle of the day, Jesus, who was tired and thirsty from traveling, met a woman at a well in Samaria. He asked the woman for a drink of water, which was very unusual because, at that time, the Samaritans and the Jews would not even speak to each other, let alone ask for some water. In addition, the woman was a sinner—an outcast. She had no hope of change because she had the same sinful nature as Adam. But Jesus knew this and wanted to share the gift of God's love, hope, and salvation with her. In the story, we find that she not only accepted Him, but many people in her village accepted Jesus too. No longer were the people hopeless. Jesus met her where she was, and hope was born. God meets us where we are too. According to the Online Merriam-Webster Dictionary, *salvation* means "deliverance from the power and effects of sin." Look at what happened according to the Scriptures.

John 4:10 (NIV), "Jesus answered her, 'If you knew the gift of God and who it is that asks you for a drink, you would have asked him and he would have given you living water.'"

John 4:13–14 (NIV), "Jesus answered, 'Everyone who drinks this water will be thirsty again, but whoever drinks the water I give them will never thirst. Indeed, the water I give them will become in them a spring of water welling up to eternal life.'"

John 7:38 (NLT), "Anyone who believes in me may come and drink! For the Scriptures declare, 'Rivers of living water will flow from his heart.'"

> *Many of the Samaritans from that town believed in him because of the woman's testimony, "He told me everything I ever did." So when the Samaritans came to him, they urged him to stay with them, and he*

> *stayed two days. And because of his words many more became believers.*
>
> *They said to the woman, "We no longer believe just because of what you said; now we have heard for ourselves, and we know that this man really is the Savior of the world."*
>
> **John 4:39–42 (NIV)**

John 6:47 (NKJV), "Most assuredly, I say to you, he who believes in Me has everlasting life."

Jesus' ministry to the Israelites and the Samaritans angered the Jewish religious and legal communities. They were afraid of losing their power and authority over the hopeless people. They did not like that He told the people there was a better way. So they decided to kill Jesus. They paid witnesses to testify against Him falsely. The false witnesses also incited the crowds who demanded Jesus be crucified. Normally, crucifixion was used for only the vilest of criminals. Jesus was not a criminal, nor was He guilty of the charges brought against Him; instead, Jesus was innocent of all the charges. But that made no difference because Father God planned to sacrifice His Son to redeem you and me from sin and death.

> *But he was pierced for our transgressions,*
>
> *he was crushed for our iniquities;*
>
> *the punishment that brought us peace was on him,*
>
> *and by his wounds we are healed.*
>
> *We all, like sheep, have gone astray,*

each of us has turned to our own way;

and the Lord has laid on him

the iniquity of us all.

Isaiah 53:5–6 (NIV)

Isaiah 53:10 (NIV), "Yet it was the Lord's will to crush him and cause him to suffer, and though the Lord makes his life an offering for sin..."

The Lord, in Isaiah 53:10, refers to Father God, who declared Jesus guilty for your sin. Therefore, Jesus died willingly for you so that you would be forgiven, considered righteous in God's eyes, and have a relationship with Him.

Second Corinthians 5:21 (NIV), "God made him who had no sin to be sin for us, so that in him we might become the righteousness of God."

A sinless man for a sinful people! Jesus brought hope to you and all the people of the world!

Let us go back to the night Jesus was falsely accused. In the middle of the night, the religious leaders held an illegal trial. Illegal because trials were to take place in the daytime. The verdict? He was declared guilty; Jesus was sentenced to immediate death by crucifixion; the soldiers beat Him until He was bloody and almost dead. They also spat on Jesus and pulled out His beard. He was mocked; a crown of thorns was placed on His head, and He was nailed to a cross for your rebellious, sinful nature. He was sinless and innocent, but He chose to take your place to make you righteous before a holy God.

According to the Online Merriam-Webster Dictionary, being *righteous* means "to be free from guilt or sin." God declared you not guilty and declared you righteous and without sin at the same time. At His death, Jesus took away Satan's dominion and power over you. Satan no longer can accuse or condemn you for your past sins if you have asked God to forgive you. Satan no longer has power over you. And that, my friend, is hope!

Romans 6:23 (NIV), "For the wages of sin is death, but the gift of God is eternal life in Christ Jesus our Lord."

> *You were dead because of your sins and because your sinful nature was not yet cut away. Then God made you alive with Christ, for he forgave all our sins. He canceled the record of the charges against us and took it away by nailing it to the cross. In this way, he disarmed the spiritual rulers and authorities. He shamed them publicly by his victory over them on the cross.*
>
> **Colossians 2:13–15 (NLT)**

Colossians 1:13–14 (NLT), "For he has rescued us from the kingdom of darkness and transferred us into the Kingdom of his dear Son, who purchased our freedom and forgave our sins." The "he" in Colossians chapter 1 refers to Father God, who rescued us from the kingdom of darkness, transferring us into the kingdom of His Son, Jesus.

In Genesis 2:7, we learned that physical life began when God breathed His breath of life into Adam and Eve.

So likewise, when Jesus breathed on the disciples, they were spiritually born again; a new spirit man, free from the bondage of sin, was born.

John 20:22 (KJV), "And when he had said this, he breathed on them, and saith unto them, Receive ye the Holy Ghost."

The Holy Spirit of God, also called the Holy Ghost, came to live in their spirit. So, likewise, when you accept Jesus, the Holy Spirit comes to live in your born-again spirit too. But let us return to that third day, also known as Resurrection Day, when Jesus rose from the dead.

On Sunday, the evening of resurrection day, Jesus appeared to His disciples and friends behind locked doors. They had been afraid of the Jewish leaders who had planned the death of Jesus. The disciples were confused because they did not know what had gone wrong. Was not Jesus supposed to be their next king? Yet He had died three days before on the cross. The women, who had gone to the tomb that morning, said they had seen Him; Jesus was alive. But where was He? Had He abandoned them? Then, suddenly, Jesus appeared in the upper room with them.

Jesus endured the punishment we deserved: death and separation from God. Then, on the third day, when the debt for all sin was satisfied, the Holy Spirit of God raised Jesus from the dead.

> *Yes, Adam's one sin brings condemnation for everyone, but Christ's one act of*

righteousness brings a right relationship with God and new life for everyone. Because one person disobeyed God, many became sinners. But because one other person obeyed God, many will be made righteous. God's law was given so that all people could see how sinful they were. But as people sinned more and more, God's wonderful grace became more abundant. So just as sin ruled over all people and brought them to death, now God's wonderful grace rules instead, giving us right standing with God and resulting in eternal life through Jesus Christ our Lord.

Romans 5:18–21 (NLT)

God's law, the Ten Commandments, was given to the people, but they could not keep it, so God sent Jesus, who brought us a new and better law: the law of love.

John 13:34 (NLT), "So now I am giving you a new commandment: Love each other. Just as I have loved you, you should love each other."

After Jesus' resurrection, He walked again on the earth for forty days, and then He ascended into heaven. The Bible tells us that Jesus was and still is seated at the right hand of the Father, interceding for each of us. But that is not all. Whoever believes in Jesus, God's Son, will have everlasting life and live with Him forever.

John 6:40 (NIV), "For my Father's will is that everyone who looks to the Son and believes in him shall have eternal life, and I will raise them up at the last day."

In this verse, we see some words that need clarification. Online Merriam-Webster Dictionary defines *will* as "a person's desire or intent regarding something." God intends that all people who believe in His Son Jesus Christ, including you, will be redeemed and brought into right standing with Him, having everlasting life. The words *everlasting life* mean "life without end." We do not know what that will look like, but we will live in God's presence forever.

Everyone refers to "all who have lived, are living, and who will live in the future, including you." Therefore, Father God desires that everyone believes in His Son, Jesus Christ. The angel Gabriel told Mary to give her baby the name Immanuel, which is translated as Jesus, because the name *Jesus* means "He will save His people."

Matthew 1:21 (NIV), "She will give birth to a son, and you are to give him the name Jesus, because he will save his people from their sins."

Jesus is also called *Jesus Christ* and is sometimes referred to as the *Christ*. Christ is not Jesus' last name but describes His title. Christ comes from the Greek word *Christos*, meaning "anointed or chosen one" (Zodhiates 1984, 1740).

Therefore, we could say that Jesus Christ is the anointed one and His anointing.

Going back to John 6:40, you need to understand the words *eternal life*, which in Greek is *Aiōnios,* defined as "the life of God that is not subject to time" (Zodhiates 1984,

1661).

As a human being, you live in a physical body that will function for a time, then cease to function, which is physical death. But, like God, you are a spirit being. So when you accept Jesus as your Savior, your physical body might die, but your spirit lives for all eternity in the presence of God.

You have free will that allows you to make choices. However, it is important to know that if you choose not to believe in and accept Jesus, your spirit still lives for eternity but is separated from God. However, you might say, "I am so bad and have sinned so much; why would God even consider forgiving me? Why would He want me in His family?" The Father's answer is, "I sent Jesus to save you!"

John 3:16 (NIV), "For God so loved the world that he gave his one and only Son, that whoever believes in him shall not perish but have eternal life."

Jesus loves you with an everlasting love that you only need to accept as a gift. God has made it easy to be part of His family, for when you choose Jesus, you are forgiven and no longer guilty of sin. God sees you through the blood that Jesus shed on the cross, making you a new person, clean and pure in God's eyes. He calls you His child and part of His family for all eternity.

Jesus asked the Samaritan woman at the well if she was thirsty. So now, He asks you the same question, "Are you thirsty?" When you drink the water Jesus gives, the Holy

Spirit comes to live in you as a well of living water.

In Genesis chapter one, we saw that God spoke all creation into existence by the word of His mouth. By the words of your mouth and the belief in your heart, you can receive His forgiveness and obtain right standing with God now.

> *If you openly declare that Jesus is Lord and believe in your heart that God raised him from the dead, you will be saved. For it is by believing in your heart that you are made right with God, and it is by openly declaring your faith that you are saved. As the Scriptures tell us, "Anyone who trusts in him will never be disgraced." Jew and Gentile are the same in this respect. They have the same Lord, who gives generously to all who call on him. For "Everyone who calls on the name of the Lord will be saved."*

> **Romans 10:9–13 (NLT)**

If you do not know Jesus as your Savior, but would like to have your sins forgiven and walk in a new life with Jesus as your Lord, pray the following prayer and ask Jesus into your life.

Father God, I have sinned, and I ask You to forgive me for all my sins. I believe that Jesus, Your Son, died on the cross for me and rose again. Therefore, Jesus, please come into my heart. Change my life into the life You have planned for me. Thank You for saving me. I ask this in Jesus' name. Amen.

If you prayed that prayer with a sincere heart, you have accepted Jesus. You are born again, forgiven, and have become spiritually baptized into Jesus Christ. Jesus now lives in your spirit. In addition, the Holy Spirit lives in you as a river of water. When you accepted Jesus as your Savior and Lord, the life and nature of God recreated you so that you have become a new creature—a new species. You have become a child of God, a member of God's family. Your sins are forgiven, and your future is settled for eternity. He will never leave you; only you can sperate yourself from His love. Your future is settled for all time; for now, you have life in the presence of God for all eternity. He will never leave you. And no one can separate you from God's love. Your future is settled for all time— you have life in the presence of God for all eternity.

CHAPTER 13:

WHY IS WATER BAPTISM IMPORTANT?

Baptism means "to immerse, to submerge" (Zodhiates 1984, 1673).

The online Merriam-Webster Dictionary defines *immersion* as "being completely covered with water." Baptism signifies cleansing from a sinful nature. For Christian believers, baptism is the outward or public declaration of a heartfelt acceptance of Jesus as their Savior and Lord, symbolizing trust and commitment to follow Him.

Jewish priests used baptism in their cleansing and purification rituals long before Christians baptized converts. For example, Old Testament Jewish priests used baptism in their ceremonial purification and cleansing before and after entering the holy of holies, also known as the Most Holy Place in the tabernacle and temple. Also, a person converting to the Jewish religion was baptized by immersing in water as part of the purification process for new converts.

In the New Testament, John the Baptist used baptism as the central sacrament of his Messianic movement. He preached repentance and remission of sins, declaring that everyone should repent and be baptized as an act of cleansing and purification from sin. John's message was to usher in the Messianic Age, also known as the Kingdom Age.

Mark 1:4–5 (NKJV), "John came baptizing in the wilderness and preaching a baptism of repentance for the remission of sins. Then all the land of Judea, and those from Jerusalem, went out to him and were all baptized by him in the Jordan River, confessing their sins."

God had promised John that He would see and recognize the Messiah before his death (John 1:29–34). So when Jesus was about thirty years old and ready to begin His public ministry, even though He was sinless, He requested John to baptize Him, fulfilling the requirements for righteousness.

> Then Jesus went from Galilee to the Jordan
> River to be baptized by John. But John tried
> to talk him out of it. "I am the one who needs
> to be baptized by you," he said, "so why
> are you coming to me?" But Jesus said, "It
> should be done, for we must carry out all that
> God requires." So John agreed to baptize
> him. After his baptism, as Jesus came up out

*of the water, the heavens were opened and
he saw the Spirit of God descending like a
dove and settling on him. And a voice from
heaven said, "This is my dearly loved Son,
who brings me great joy."*

Matthew 3:13–17 (NLT)

Jesus' baptism confirmed God's promise to John to see
and recognize the Messiah before His death. After Jesus
rose from the water, the heavens opened. The people
heard the voice of God calling Jesus His beloved Son.
Immediately, John knew Jesus was the Messiah. So John
called Jesus the Lamb that Isaiah had prophecized would
be slaughtered (Isaiah 53:7).

*The next day John saw Jesus coming toward
him and said, "Look, the Lamb of God, who
takes away the sin of the world! This is the
one I meant when I said, 'A man who comes
after me has surpassed me because he was
before me.' I myself did not know him, but the
reason I came baptizing with water was that
he might be revealed to Israel." Then John
gave this testimony: "I saw the Spirit come
down from heaven as a dove and remain on
him. And I myself did not know him, but the
one who sent me to baptize with water told
me, 'The man on whom you see the Spirit
come down and remain is the one who will
baptize with the Holy Spirit.' I have seen and
I testify that this is God's Chosen One."*

John 1:29–34 (NIV)

About three years later, before ascending into heaven, Jesus gave His disciples some last instructions.

> *Then Jesus came to them and said, "All authority in heaven and on earth has been given to me. Therefore go and make disciples of all nations, baptizing them in the name of the Father and of the Son and of the Holy Spirit, and teaching them to obey everything I have commanded you. And surely I am with you always, to the very end of the age."*
>
> **Matthew 28:18–20 (NIV)**

Jesus commanded all disciples of Jesus Christ to be baptized in the name of the Father, the Son, and the Holy Spirit (Matthew 28:19). A *disciple* is "anyone who is born again and a follower of Jesus Christ." Paul taught the church in Rome how to be disciples.

Romans 10:9–10 (NIV), "If you declare with your mouth, 'Jesus is Lord,' and believe in your heart that God raised him from the dead, you will be saved. For it is with your heart that you believe and are justified, and it is with your mouth that you profess your faith and are saved."

Even though water baptism is one of the church's ordinances, it is also a public commitment of faith in Jesus Christ. Baptism does not save you but declares that you have been saved by faith in God's Son Jesus.

> *But because of his great love for us, God, who is rich in mercy, made us alive with Christ even when we were dead in transgressions —it is by grace you have been saved. And*

God raised us up with Christ and seated us with him in the heavenly realms in Christ Jesus, in order that in the coming ages he might show the incomparable riches of his grace, expressed in his kindness to us in Christ Jesus. For it is by grace you have been saved, through faith —and this is not from yourselves, it is the gift of God—not by works, so that no one can boast.

Ephesians 2:4–9 (NIV)

So why should you be baptized in water? Because baptism shows your identification with Jesus Christ as you renounce sin and declare your faith in Him. It symbolizes that you have chosen to follow Jesus. Water baptism represents your death to sin, and you are cleansed of all unrighteousness. Rising from the water suggests that you have been raised from death with Christ. So we could say that baptism shows that you have died to sin, been made alive in Christ, and are now walking in a new life.

Galatians 2:20 (NIV), "I have been crucified with Christ and I no longer live, but Christ lives in me. The life I now live in the body, I live by faith in the Son of God, who loved me and gave himself for me."

Jesus was crucified and died for you, but on the third day, He arose and lives forever. When you are baptized, it symbolizes that you and your sin died with Him, and you rose to a new life in Him. You will live forever in the presence of God—on earth and in heaven when you pass from this earth.

> *Or do you not know that as many of us as were*
> *baptized into Christ Jesus were baptized into*
> *His death? Therefore we were buried with*
> *Him through baptism into death, that just as*
> *Christ was raised from the dead by the glory*
> *of the Father, even so we also should walk in*
> *newness of life.*

Romans 6:3–4 (NKJV)

Paul told believers at Ephesus who were called by God to be born again that baptism is one of the things that unifies the body of Christ.

> *As a prisoner for the Lord, then, I urge you*
> *to live a life worthy of the calling you have*
> *received. Be completely humble and gentle;*
> *be patient, bearing with one another in love.*
> *Make every effort to keep the unity of the*
> *Spirit through the bond of peace. There is one*
> *body and one Spirit, just as you were called*
> *to one hope when you were called; one Lord,*
> *one faith, one baptism; one God and Father*
> *of all, who is over all and through all and*
> *in all. But to each one of us grace has been*
> *given as Christ apportioned it.*

Ephesians 4:1–7 (NIV)

Baptism cannot save you; only accepting Jesus will save you from the sinful nature you had. At the cross, one of the criminals hanging next to Jesus realized that he was a sinner and asked Jesus to remember him. Jesus acknowledged his repentance and forgave him. Jesus said, "You will be with Me today," indicating that the man had been forgiven by Jesus. He received eternal life. He never experienced water baptism, but at that moment, he was spiritually baptized into Christ and raised to eternal life by the power of Jesus' word.

> *One of the criminals hanging beside him scoffed, "So you're the Messiah, are you? Prove it by saving yourself—and us, too, while you're at it!"*
>
> *But the other criminal protested, "Don't you fear God even when you have been sentenced to die? We deserve to die for our crimes, but this man hasn't done anything wrong." Then he said, "Jesus, remember me when you come into your Kingdom." And Jesus replied, "I assure you, today you will be with me in paradise."*

Luke 23:39–43 (NLT)

THERE ARE SEVERAL TYPES OF BAPTISMS:

1. *Baptism into Christ.* We are baptized into Christ when we are born again. This is a spiritual baptism where Christ Jesus comes to live in your spirit. There is no water involved.

2. *Baptism by immersion in water.* We have just discussed this type of baptism, which represents our death to sin and being cleansed from all unrighteousness that leads to a new life in Christ Jesus.

3. *Baptism by sprinkling.* Baptism by sprinkling is used commonly in infant baptism. From Adam's

fall from grace by disobedience, everyone is born with the original sin nature. Although baptism cannot save a person, many denominations use baptism to symbolize inclusion into the covenant.

Many families have a dedication service for their infants in some denominations instead of infant baptism. The parents, grandparents, and friends dedicate the infant to the Lord, committing themselves to raise the child in a godly way, teaching them to love and honor the Lord. Infants are too young to speak for themselves; therefore, the family and friends commit to following the Lord's commands and statutes on behalf of the children. However, a person who has been baptized or dedicated as an infant still must choose to accept and follow Jesus Christ, repenting of their sin before they are saved and enter into eternal life with God.

Under the Old Testament, the sign of the covenant was used for inclusion in the covenant. The sign was not baptism but circumcision. God required every male infant eight days old to be circumcised in the flesh to be included in the Abrahamic Covenant (Genesis 17:9–14). The number eight symbolizes a new beginning; the old has passed away, and the new begins. However, infant baptism does not wash away any original sin or save the child from their sinful nature. Once again, many denominations believe that infant baptism includes the child in the parent's covenant with God. Paul clears this up when He connects circumcision with baptism when teaching the Colossians (Colossians 2:11–15). He teaches that we are baptized without hands into Christ as New Testament believers in Christ. This is spiritual baptism.

Romans 2:29 (NLT), "And true circumcision is not merely obeying the letter of the law; rather, it is a change of heart produced by the Spirit. And a person with a changed heart seeks praise from God, not from people."

> *For you are all children of God through faith in Christ Jesus. And all who have been united with Christ in baptism have put on Christ, like putting on new clothes. There is no longer Jew or Gentile, slave or free, male and female. For you are all one in Christ Jesus. And now that you belong to Christ, you are the true children of Abraham. You are his heirs, and God's promise to Abraham belongs to you.*
>
> **Galatians 3:26–29 (NLT)**

The reference to being united with Christ in baptism refers to spiritual baptism, not water baptism.

4 *Other sprinkling baptisms.* Sometimes sprinkling is used for adults instead of immersion. Some examples would be when a person is near death or too ill to be immersed in water or no water is readily available such as on a battlefield.

5 *The baptism of the Holy Spirit.* This baptism happens after a person is born again and has the Holy Spirit living in them. The Baptism of the Holy Spirit is a spiritual baptism to receive the power of the Holy Spirit in their life for ministering as the Holy Spirit chooses.

CHAPTER 14:

WHAT IS THE BAPTISM OF THE HOLY SPIRIT?

Acts 1:8 (NIV), "But you will receive power when the Holy Spirit comes on you; and you will be my witnesses in Jerusalem, and in all Judea and Samaria, and to the ends of the earth."

Once you are born again, the Holy Spirit, also known as the Spirit of Christ, comes to live in you as a well of living water. However, to receive the baptism of the Holy Spirit, you have to ask the Father in the name of Jesus. When you are baptized in the Holy Spirit, your witness of Jesus increases. The power of the Holy Spirit in you becomes like a stream of living water flowing from you to others.

Let us look in the Scriptures to see how others received the baptism of the Holy Spirit. These other events show that baptism and speaking in tongues were not isolated events in the New Testament. Let us begin with Philip, one of the original apostles.

> *The next day Jesus decided to leave for Galilee. Finding Philip, he said to him, "Follow me." Philip, like Andrew and Peter, was from the town of Bethsaida. Philip found Nathanael and told him, "We have found the one Moses wrote about in the Law, and about whom the prophets also wrote —Jesus of Nazareth, the son of Joseph."*
>
> **John 1:43–45 (NIV)**

Philip, an evangelist, was not brought to Jesus by another apostle; rather, Jesus found Philip and invited Philip to join Him as a disciple. Then Philip brought Nathanael to Jesus. From the scriptures in John 1:44, we know that Philip was a devout man who loved God. History tells us that Phillip had four daughters who were preachers and that Paul loved to stay in his home. In addition, his preaching was effective in bringing others to Jesus.

> *Philip went down to the city of Samaria and began proclaiming Christ to them. The crowds with one accord were giving attention to what was said by Philip, as they heard and saw the signs which he was performing. For in the case of many who had unclean spirits, they were coming out of them shouting with a loud voice; and many who had been paralyzed and lame were healed. So there was much rejoicing in that city. But when*

they believed Philip preaching the good news about the kingdom of God and the name of Jesus Christ, they were being baptized, men and women alike.

Acts 8:5–8, 12 (NASB)

Now when the apostles in Jerusalem heard that Samaria had received the word of God, they sent them Peter and John, who came down and prayed for them that they might receive the Holy Spirit. For He had not yet fallen upon any of them; they had simply been baptized in the name of the Lord Jesus. Then they began laying their hands on them, and they were receiving the Holy Spirit.

Acts 8:14–17 (NASB)

These Samaritans believed in and accepted Jesus—they were born again. So when Peter and John came, they did not pray for them to be saved but that they might receive the fullness of the baptism of the Holy Spirit.

Another example is the apostle Peter, whom God sent to minister to a Gentile named Cornelius. In Acts 10, we find the story of Cornelius, a centurion in the Italian regiment. His family members were devout God-fearing people, although they were not Jews. The Holy Spirit instructed Peter to go to Cornelius' home, where his family and a large gathering waited. Peter spoke to them about Jesus. While he was speaking, the Holy Spirit came on all who heard the message. There is no mention of anyone laying hands on Cornelius while listening to Peter talk about

191

Jesus. But they all received the baptism of the Holy Spirit. Peter and the believers with Peter heard them speaking in tongues and magnifying God, which is the evidence of receiving the baptism of the Holy Spirit. They were born again, and they received the baptism of the Holy Spirit at the same time, even though they were not Jews. Then they were baptized in water. The gifts of salvation and the Holy Spirit are free for everyone.

The prophet Joel spoke about the Holy Spirit being poured out or given to anyone who desired the power of God.

> *And afterward,*
>
> *I will pour out my Spirit on all people.*
>
> *Your sons and daughters will prophesy,*
>
> *your old men will dream dreams,*
>
> *your young men will see visions.*
>
> *Even on my servants, both men and women,*
>
> *I will pour out my Spirit in those days.*
>
> **Joel 2:28–29 (NIV)**

Let us see another example of receiving the Holy Spirit, but this time with the laying on of hands:

> *While Apollos was at Corinth, Paul took the road through the interior and arrived at Ephesus. There he found some disciples and asked them, "Did you receive the Holy Spirit when you believed?" They answered, "No, we have not even heard that there is a Holy Spirit." So Paul asked, "Then what baptism did you*

receive?"

"John's baptism," they replied.

Paul said, "John's baptism was a baptism of repentance. He told the people to believe in the one coming after him, that is, in Jesus." On hearing this, they were baptized in the name of the Lord Jesus. When Paul placed his hands on them, the Holy Spirit came on them, and they spoke in tongues and prophesied.

Acts 19:1–6 (NIV)

In every instance, people who were born again received the Holy Spirit with evidence of speaking in other tongues whether or not hands were laid on them. Notice no one was denied. And they all spoke in tongues when they received. Do you want to receive the baptism of the Holy Spirit? To receive the power of God, the baptism of the Holy Spirit, you have to ask, receive, then use your voice to speak out the words He gives you. There are over seven thousand languages in the world. The Holy Spirit can and does use words from many languages. The Holy Spirit chooses what words to impart to you as your special prayer language.

At first, it may sound weird to you, but that is okay. You are so special that He can trust you to use the words He has assigned to you as you worship and magnify God. As you use the words He gives you, more words will come. These words are your spiritual prayer language so you can speak directly to God. Prayer is simply talking to God, just like you talk to a friend.

Remember the Holy Spirit gives you the words to say; you provide your voice to the Holy Spirit to speak the words. Do not be afraid. The Holy Spirit is always a gentleman, and He will never embarrass you. God wants you to have this special new prayer language that helps you worship and speak mysteries to God. This special language also enables you to pray when you do not know how or what to pray, and it helps you move deeper into worship. When using tongues during prayer, it is commonly called "praying in the Spirit." It is all right to pray in your natural language or your new spiritual language anytime you choose.

The Holy Spirit is a gift from God our Father to take Jesus' place on earth after Jesus returned to heaven. The Holy Spirit comforts you, teaches you, and guides you. The baptism of the Holy Spirit is like a river of water flowing from God through you to others; it is a supernatural release of the power of the Holy Spirit that enables you to be a witness for Jesus. Once again, look at Acts 1:8.

Acts 1:8 (NASB), "But you will receive power when the Holy Spirit has come upon you; and you shall be My witnesses both in Jerusalem, and in all Judea and Samaria, and even to the remotest part of the earth."

This power does not change who you are or make you do or say something wrong. Instead, this supernatural power of the Holy Spirit gives you an understanding of the circumstances, the ability, and the words to minister to others. Look at Acts 2:1–6 to see how Father God sent the Holy Spirit to Jesus' disciples.

When the day of Pentecost had come, they were all together in one place. And suddenly there came from heaven a noise like a violent rushing wind, and it filled the whole house where they were sitting. And there appeared to them tongues as of fire distributing themselves, and they rested on each one of them. And they were all filled with the Holy Spirit and began to speak with other tongues, as the Spirit was giving them utterance. Now there were Jews living in Jerusalem, devout men from every nation under heaven. And when this sound occurred, the crowd came together, and were bewildered because each one of them was hearing them speak in his own language.

Acts 2:1–6 (NASB)

Notice the crowd at the feast of Pentecost heard the sound of the wind. They heard Jesus' disciples and other followers speaking in languages that were not their native language. The crowd was from many places, not just Jerusalem, and the people in the crowd heard them speaking in languages they could understand. The evidence of receiving the baptism of the Holy Spirit is speaking in other tongues that are not your native language.

I was raised in a Christian home and accepted Jesus as my Savior when I was twelve years old. My father was a deacon in the church, and my mother taught Sunday school. We went to church for every service or activity. I knew the usual Bible stories, but I did not understand the Bible. As an adult, after I received the baptism of the

Holy Spirit, I began to understand the many truths of the Bible. I read and understood what God's Word was saying to me.

Many people misunderstand the baptism of the Holy Spirit and speaking in tongues. Some say it was only for the original apostles or that it is of the devil. But neither of those sayings is true. As you continue to read and study the book of Acts, you will see the power of the Holy Spirit at work in those who were ministering to others. God intended for the Holy Spirit to live in us for our benefit and flow out of us with supernatural power to help others. The Online Merriam-Webster Dictionary defines *supernatural* as "departing from the usual and normal. The supernatural appears to transcend the laws of nature."

Go back to Acts 2:3–4 to see some additional information.

Acts 2:3–4 (NKJV), "And there appeared to them tongues as of fire distributing themselves, and they rested on each one of them. And they were all filled with the Holy Spirit and began to speak with other tongues, as the Spirit was giving them utterance."

In these verses, we are told that tongues of fire sat on each of them. After the exodus from Egypt, in the Old Testament book of Exodus, the Holy Spirit came in a cloud by day and fire by night, covering and protecting the Israelites as they traveled through the wilderness. But in the book of Acts, the Holy Spirit came like tongues of fire that sat on each apostle.

Fire has many purposes. It can destroy, purify, produce heat and light, produce energy, and consume everything in its path. For example, God appeared to Moses in a burning bush when He called Moses to lead the children of Israel out of Egypt, but the fire did not consume the bush.

Exodus 3:2 (NKJV), "And the Angel of the Lord appeared to him in a flame of fire from the midst of a bush. So he looked, and behold, the bush was burning with fire, but the bush was not consumed."

Born as a Hebrew, Moses had been protected from the Pharoah's command to kill all babies under two years old. To save him, when Moses was three months old, his mother put him in a basket and placed the basket in the river where Pharoah's daughter bathed each day. She took him home when she found him and raised him as her son. Moses was given the best education the courts of the Pharoah provided. One day, forty-year-old Moses witnessed an Egyptian slave master mistreating a Hebrew worker. Moses was very angry, so he killed the slave master. With a death contract on his life for murder, Moses fled to the desert of Midian.

After forty years in the desert of Midian, Moses, who was eighty years old, was approached by God in a burning bush, but the fire did not consume the bush. God told Moses that he was to lead the children of Israel out of Egypt, where they had been held hostage for four hundred years in slavery and bondage. Moses and his brother Aaron traveled to Egypt, where they confronted the Pharaoh. The Pharaoh's refusal to let the people leave resulted in God sending ten plagues on the Egyptians. Finally, the Pharaoh released the people. While they were leaving Egypt, God supernaturally parted the water of the Red Sea, permitting the people to cross on dry land. Then they traveled through the wilderness to the foot of Mount Sinai, where they camped for many months. Frequently, the fire of God rested on the mountain resulting in a frightful scene to the children of Israel.

Exodus 24:17 (NKJV), "The sight of the glory of the Lord was like a consuming fire on the top of the mountain in the eyes of the children of Israel."

Hebrews 12:29 (NASB), "For our God is a consuming fire."

Let us go back to the tongues of fire on the day of Pentecost in Acts 1:8. They represented the glory and presence of God, which produces energy, power, and heat but does not consume or destroy. In the natural, fire can be comfortable when sitting nearby on a cold night, or it can purify the fields for planting, or it can be the fire of passion for completing an assignment or job that you stay up all night to finish. It can be the fire or passion of new love, the birth of a long-awaited child, or seeing a loved one you have not seen in many years. Fire has many forms, but the fire of the Holy Spirit is the fire that produces the power of God in you to fulfill His plans in your life.

Speaking in tongues is the initial sign of having received the baptism of the Holy Spirit.

> *And there were dwelling in Jerusalem Jews,*
> *devout men, from every nation under heaven.*
> *And when this sound occurred, the multitude*
> *came together, and were confused, because*
> *everyone heard them speak in his own*
> *language. Then they were all amazed and*
> *marveled, saying to one another, "Look, are*
> *not all these who speak Galileans? And how*
> *is it that we hear, each in our own language*
> *in which we were born?"*

Acts 2:5–8 (NKJV)

Notice all those assembled with the disciples were filled with the Holy Spirit and began to speak in other tongues. Speaking with other tongues means the language spoken is not the person's native language and is unknown to that person. The Bible gives us more insight into this unusual experience of unknown languages or tongues. So let us take a side journey to the time of Noah to help us understand tongues.

Genesis 10:32 (NIV), "These are the clans of Noah's sons, according to their lines of descent, within their nations. From these the nations spread out over the earth after the flood."

Genesis 11:1 (NIV), "Now the whole world had one language and a common speech."

As the people settled in various places, some settled in Shinar, another name for Babylon. The people had become rebellious towards God, so they decided to build a tower reaching the heavens to make a name for themselves. But God was watching this and knew that they could accomplish anything when the people got together and spoke the same language. So He disbursed them throughout the nations and confused their language (Genesis 11:1–9).

First Corinthians 14:10 (NLT), "There are many different languages in the world, and every language has meaning."

Once there was only one language. Now, Ethnologue, a company that keeps records of languages, reported that in 2021 there were 7,139 languages spoken in the world. These numbers do not include computer and internet languages (Eberhard 2021).

The Holy Spirit uses all these languages in whatever form He chooses to enable people to speak in tongues. So let's see how the Holy Spirit uses tongues.

1. Speaking in tongues is a way to worship and praise God.

   While Peter was still speaking these words, the Holy Spirit came on all who heard the message. The circumcised believers who had come with Peter were astonished that the gift of the Holy Spirit had been poured out even on Gentiles. For they heard them speaking in tongues and praising God.

   Acts 10:44–46 (NIV)

Many times, we are so filled with love for God that we cannot find words in our natural languages to speak. As we worship God, the Holy Spirit gives us other words to say that are not our usual words. The Holy Spirit knows the heart and mind of God and uses us to speak those words.

2. Speaking in tongues does not speak to men but God.

First Corinthians 14:2–3 (NIV), "For anyone who speaks in a tongue does not speak to people but to God. Indeed, no one understands them; they utter mysteries by the Spirit. But the one who prophesies speaks to people for their strengthening, encouragement, and comfort."

3. The Holy Spirit prays for us when we pray in tongues.

First Corinthians 14:14–15 (NIV), "For if I pray in a tongue, my spirit prays, but my mind is unfruitful. So what shall I do? I will pray with my spirit, but I will also pray with my understanding."

Did you ever even think you could speak directly to God in a spiritual language? Well, you can when you receive the baptism of the Holy Spirit.

4. Speaking in tongues edifies the person speaking and others.

First Corinthians 14:4 (NIV), "Anyone who speaks in a tongue edifies themselves, but the one who prophesies edifies the church."

Jude 1:20–21 (NLT), "But you, dear friends, must build each other up in your most holy faith, pray in

201

the power of the Holy Spirit, and await the mercy of our Lord Jesus Christ, who will bring you eternal life. In this way, you will keep yourselves safe in God's love."

Are you discouraged? Are you lonely? Speaking or praying in tongues, also known as praying in the Spirit, can change your emotions, causing you to feel happy and hopeful. The circumstances may not change, but speaking or praying in the Spirit changes how you respond to them.

5. Speaking in tongues is a sign for unbelievers.

Therefore tongues are for a sign, not to those who believe but to unbelievers; but prophesying is not for unbelievers but for those who believe. Therefore if the whole church comes together in one place, and all speak with tongues, and there come in those who are uninformed or unbelievers, will they not say that you are out of your mind? But if all prophesy, and an unbeliever or an uninformed person comes in, he is convinced by all, he is convicted by all. And thus the secrets of his heart are revealed; and so, falling down on his face, he will worship God and report that God is truly among you.

1 Corinthians 14:22–25 (NKJV)

6. Speaking in tongues can be an answer to prayer.

First Corinthians 14:27 (NKJV), "If anyone speaks in a tongue, let there be two or at the most three, each in turn, and let one interpret."

According to these scriptures, it should be interpreted when a message is given in tongues. However, some years ago, I was in a church service when a message in tongues was given in the French language. I do not speak or understand French, but I recognized the language. Unfortunately, no one interpreted the message, and the service continued. After the service, several of us were speaking with our pastor when a man with a French accent came over to the group. He told us the message had been an answer to prayer for him. He had been traveling and praying about some direction he needed, and the tongues message gave him that direction.

7. Tongues are part of the Great Commission.

   Mark 16:17 (NKJV), "And these signs will follow those who believe they will speak with new tongues."

   As you can see by these scriptures, speaking in tongues is used to edify, build up your own and another's faith, talk to God, and magnify and worship God. You can use tongues when you pray, especially when you do not know how to pray. Tongues are also a sign for unbelievers when the Holy Spirit uses their native language to give them a message, or it can be an answer to someone's prayers.

   If you are born again and want the power of the

Holy Spirit in your life, ask the Father to baptize you with His Spirit, then receive the gift from God. Your special language may be only one strange word at the beginning. But use your voice to speak it out. The more you speak, the more words the Holy Spirit will give you. Do not be embarrassed. Even babies begin with sounds and only a word or two when they talk. You will need to put your pride aside and expect the words to come.

CHAPTER 15:

WHAT DOES IT MEAN TO BE IN CHRIST?

Paul revealed what it means to be in Christ to the Colossians, the Galatians, and you.

Colossians 1:26–27 (NKJV), "The mystery which has been hidden from ages and from generations, but now has been revealed to His saints. To them God willed to make known what are the riches of the glory of this mystery among the Gentiles: which is Christ in you, the hope of glory."

Galatians 3:26–28 (NIV), "So in Christ Jesus you are all children of God through faith, for all of you who were baptized into Christ have clothed yourselves with Christ. There is neither Jew nor Gentile, neither slave nor free, nor is there male and female, for you are all one in Christ Jesus."

The Scriptures tell us that you were clothed and baptized

into Christ when you accepted Jesus as your Savior. You were spiritually born again—you became a new creation. Jesus died and took your sins on Himself. As far as God is concerned, your past sins are forgiven forever. He sees you *through* the blood of Jesus. In addition, now God sees you as His child—His son or daughter. Can you comprehend the fact that you are a child of Almighty God? That you are clean and holy in His eyes? That your past is no longer an issue with God, and God is not mad at you?

Second Corinthians 5:17 (TLB), "When someone becomes a Christian, he becomes a brand-new person inside. He is not the same anymore. A new life has begun."

Second Corinthians 5:21 (TLB), "For God took the sinless Christ and poured into Him our sins. Then, in exchange, He poured God's goodness into us."

God took your sins and poured them into Jesus so that you could be free from sin. Then God poured Himself— His love and goodness—into you. He sees you as a new person, a new creation—not like you used to be. And on top of that, He calls you His child! His glory shines through each child of God.

Just as Jesus Christ is in the Father and the Father is in Jesus, Jesus Christ is in you, and you are in Jesus Christ. How awesome is that? When you decide to accept Jesus, you not only have Jesus Christ living in you, but you are in Jesus Christ. In the book of John, we hear Jesus talking to His disciples about this very same thing.

John 14:10–11 (NLT), "Don't you believe that I am in

the Father and the Father is in me? The words I speak are not my own, but my Father who lives in me does his work through me. Just believe that I am in the Father and the Father is in me."

John 14:20 (NLT), "When I am raised to life again, you will know that I am in my Father, and you are in me, and I am in you."

In the book of Exodus, Moses met with God on Mount Sinai. He stayed on the mountain for forty days and forty nights. When he came down from the mountain, the glory of God was on Moses's face so bright he had to cover his face with a veil (Exodus 34:28–35). Unfortunately, the people could not see past the veil. Moses had received the Ten Commandments from God, but the people did not understand what God was doing for them. Only Jesus could remove the veil with His death, burial, and resurrection. When you accepted Jesus, the veil was removed for you.

Second Corinthians 3:18 (NLT), "So all of us who have had that veil removed can see and reflect the glory of the Lord. And the Lord—who is the Spirit—makes us more and more like him as we are changed into his glorious image."

Second Corinthians 4:16 (NKJV), "Even though our outward man is perishing, yet the inward man is being renewed day by day."

The Online Merriam-Webster Dictionary defines *perish* as "to become destroyed or ruined; cease to exist, to cause to die."

Your physical body, called your outward man, perishes over time, causing physical death. However, your inner-man, called your spirit-man, lives forever.

Remember, in everything, there is a God-side and a man-side. The God-side was Jesus taking all your sin on Himself, causing you to be a new creation called a Christian—a follower of Jesus Christ. You are a new species that is the home to the very Holy Spirit of God. Until Jesus died, there was no other creation that could be the home of God. In addition, if you are spiritually born again when you leave this earth, your spirit-man will live eternally in the presence of God. Being a new creation or species is not a weird science fiction experience but a true supernatural fact. Also, as a Christian, you reflect the inner glory of Jesus as you grow more like Him every day. People can see the glory of God in and on you because the power of God has changed you. You are holy not by what you wear or do but because you belong to Jesus. You are holy because God is holy.

Leviticus 11:44 (NKJV), "For I am the Lord your God. You shall therefore consecrate yourselves, and you shall be holy; for I am holy."

As a new species, you are now the dwelling place or temple of the Holy Spirit. When Jesus was instructing His disciples regarding His death, He told them He would not leave them without help; instead, the Father would give them another comforter, just like Himself, to help them and live in them. That helper and comforter is none other than the Holy Spirit, the Spirit of Christ—the third member of the Trinity. Therefore, how you live and conduct yourself shows your relationship with Jesus.

Now you understand what it means to be born again by accepting Jesus as your Savior and Lord and being a child of God. So then, let us answer your question. Who am I?

Ephesians 2:10 (NKJV), "For we are His workmanship, created in Christ Jesus for good works, which God prepared beforehand that we should walk in them."

Let us look at this scripture closely. The word *His* is placed first in Greek to bring emphasis to God. You are first and foremost His workmanship or His handiwork. You are not your own handiwork but His most precious and important masterpiece. He created you to be special. You are His beautiful creation, unlike any other creation. You might say, "Well, flowers are more beautiful!" They are beautiful, but they cannot love Him as you can love Him. You might say, "Well, the mountains are majestic." They are, but they cannot talk with Him as you can. They cannot be His arms that hold you when you are hurting or His eyes that watch over you—His child. Nothing else in nature could fulfill His desire to have a family. Only human beings can do that. When God looks at you, He sees the glory of God in and through you, bringing light in the darkness. He sees Christ and all His glory in you—hope for the world. He sees the Holy Spirit working through you as you touch others with the kindness and goodness of God. Know that God created you for His pleasure and purpose as you think about this wonder.

Let us continue to look at Ephesians 2:10. The word

workmanship in the Greek Dictionary is *poiema,* which means "something that is made, a creation, a work of art." You are God's work of art! Can you picture yourself as a costly, precious work of art? There is no piece of art hanging in the most famous art galleries that can compare to you in Christ.

God uses the many colors of your skin, hair, and eyes, the colors of your veins, arteries, and organs, to weave a multicolored tapestry or paint a priceless work of art called you. You are priceless in God's eyes.

The word *poiema* is also the root word for *poetry.* You tell a different and unique story that only you can tell. God is the poet who created you as a poem for the world to hear—a beautiful poem of love, joy, and peace. You are God's beautiful poetry in motion!

Go back to Ephesians 2:10. The words *in advance* carry the theme of "God's purpose and plan for you." God created you from the beginning of time for His purposes. God has planned special projects and assignments called "good works" that only you can accomplish. He gave you the skill, ability, and desire to complete the tasks He gives you. And He will see them to completion.

> *For I know the thoughts that I think toward you, says the Lord, thoughts of peace and not of evil, to give you a future and a hope. Then you will call upon Me and go and pray to Me, and I will listen to you. And you will seek Me and find Me, when you search for Me with all your heart.*
>
> **Jeremiah 29:11–13 (NKJV)**

Many people think that God could not possibly use them because of their past mistakes. That's not true. No sin or perceived failure is too great for God to forgive and use for His glory! The apostle Paul was a murderer of Christians. Except for the mercy of God, Paul would have been just another Pharisee, and we would not have known him. God knew Paul from before the foundation of the world. God knew that Paul would be the person who would write much of the New Testament, teaching us who God is and who God made us be. I love what He told the church in Rome—it applies to you too.

Romans 8:1–2 (NLT), "So now there is no condemnation for those who belong to Christ Jesus. And because you belong to him, the power of the life-giving Spirit has freed you from the power of sin that leads to death."

In Romans 8:1, you can see that when you accept Jesus, you belong to Christ; there is no condemnation. *Condemnation* means "being declared wrong, to be pronounced guilty, to be convicted, or to be censured." Because of Jesus' sacrifice for you, you are no longer condemned for your sin. Jesus took all your sins on Himself—He paid the price for you—once and for all.

> *You were dead in sins, and your sinful desires were not yet cut away. Then He gave you a share in the very life of Christ, for He forgave all your sins. And blotted out the charges proved against you, and the list of His commandments which you had not obeyed. He took this list of sins and destroyed it by nailing it to Christ's cross. In this way God*

211

*took away Satan's power to accuse you of sin,
and God openly displayed to the whole world
Christ's triumph at the cross where your sins
were all taken away.*

Colossians 2:13–15 (TLB)

God took all of your sins and nailed them to Jesus' cross so that you could be free from condemnation and guilt. Satan tries to tell you that you are still guilty, but he is a liar. God pardoned and declared you *not* guilty. You can live in peace as you submit to God and resist the devil when you are in Christ. You can know that you no longer have to live under the condemnation of your past mistakes. Jesus stripped Satan, also known as the devil, of his power and authority over you. Look at what James, Jesus' half-brother, said.

James 4:7–8 (NKJV), "Therefore submit to God. Resist the devil and he will flee from you. Draw near to God and He will draw near to you."

As a child of God, you can resist the devil, and he must flee from you. *Flee* means "to run away from danger." Is not that interesting? Without Jesus, you are not dangerous to the devil. However, when you accept Jesus Christ as your Savior, the devil runs from you because he knows Jesus triumphed over him, taking away all of his authority over you. Therefore, when you resist the devil, in Jesus' name, he must *go*!

Here is something else to think about: when you are in Christ, the Holy Spirit leads you as you learn to hear His voice by reading the Holy Bible, praying, and listening with your *spiritual ears* to what He is saying. He speaks to you in and through your spirit—your inner man. When He speaks to you, you just know that you know something.

You might ask, "How do I pray?" Prayer is not complicated; you talk to God and listen when He speaks to you. His voice always lines up with His Word. Look what the apostle Paul told the church at Philippi.

> *Don't worry about anything; instead, pray about everything. Tell God what you need, and thank him for all he has done. Then you will experience God's peace, which exceeds anything we can understand. His peace will guard your hearts and minds as you live in Christ Jesus.*
>
> **Philippians 4:6–7 (NLT)**

Everyone tries to do things their own way, with their own ability, but they fail at some point in their life. However, when you are in Christ, you have the power of the Holy Spirit available at all times to help you. You do not have to do everything by yourself anymore.

Zechariah 4:6 (NKJV), "This is the word of the Lord to Zerubbabel: 'Not by might nor by power, but by My Spirit,' Says the Lord of hosts."

You might ask, "How do I access the power of the Holy Spirit?" You talk to the Holy Spirit just as you would a friend, asking Him in Jesus' name for His help. The apostle John teaches us to *abide* in Jesus and His Word.

John 15:7 (NKJV), "If you abide in Me, and My words

abide in you, you will ask what you desire, and it shall be done for you."

Menō, the word for *abide,* means "to remain, to live with, to dwell." (Zodhiates 1984, 1710 #3306) If you stay or reside in God's Word, it becomes truth to you. Then, you can trust and rely on His Word. However, James teaches that wisdom, faith, and common sense are also needed to access the power of the Holy Spirit and the other promises of God.

> *If any of you lacks wisdom, let him ask of God, who gives to all liberally and without reproach, and it will be given to him. But let him ask in faith, with no doubting, for he who doubts is like a wave of the sea driven and tossed by the wind. For let not that man suppose that he will receive anything from the Lord; he is a double-minded man, unstable in all his ways.*
>
> **James 1:5–8 (NKJV)**

Go with me back to the book of Mark, then to the book of Matthew to see how Jesus teaches His disciples to pray.

> *...he says. Therefore I say to you, whatever things you ask when you pray, believe that you receive them, and you will have them. "And whenever you stand praying, if you have anything against anyone, forgive him, that your Father in heaven may also forgive you your trespasses. But if you do not forgive, neither will your Father in heaven forgive your trespasses."*
>
> **Mark 11:23–26 (NKJV)**

Matthew 7:7–8 (NKJV), "Ask, and it will be given to you; seek, and you will find; knock, and it will be opened to you. For everyone who asks receives, and he who seeks finds, and to him who knocks it will be opened."

God wants you to use your faith in Him and His kind of faith when you ask Him for your needs and desires. So many times, people do not ask God for anything because they feel guilty or not worthy. Remember you are forgiven! Your past is just that—the past. God has declared you not guilty!

And remember, when you are in Christ, you are worthy not because of what you have or have not done but because Jesus took your place when He died for you. You are worthy because Jesus is worthy! God, our Father, sees you through the sinless blood of Jesus Christ, and He sees you worthy to receive all of His blessings. Look what Jesus told His disciples in John 16:23–24 about asking for their needs and desires.

John 16:23–24 (NKJV), "And in that day you will ask Me nothing. Most assuredly, I say to you, whatever you ask the Father in My name He will give you. Until now you have asked nothing in My name. Ask, and you will receive, that your joy may be full."

If this were not enough, Paul tells us in Ephesians 2:6 that we sit with Jesus at the right hand of Father God in Christ. Now, you ask, "How can that be? I live on earth." I do not know how this is possible because it is supernatural. But God's Word says it is true, so I choose to believe it. Remember God never lies! Only by faith can you understand God's Word, not by what you see, feel, or experience.

> *But God is so rich in mercy, and he loved us so much, that even though we were dead because of our sins, he gave us life when he raised Christ from the dead. (It is only by God's grace that you have been saved!) For he raised us from the dead along with Christ and seated us with him in the heavenly realms because we are united with Christ Jesus.*

Ephesians 2:4–6 (NLT)

Consider how much God loves and trusts you! He has spiritually seated you at His right hand with Jesus. When someone is sitting at someone's right hand, it is a place of honor! God has honored you just as He honored Jesus. All I can say is, "Wow!"

For over a year, three times each week, I sat under the "in Christ" teaching. Finally, when I began to teach, I asked the Lord to help me teach this very important but complicated message in just a few minutes. As I was praying, the Holy Spirit said, "Get the bear." Immediately, I knew what He meant. When my first grandson was born, he was given a five-foot-tall, plush, brown teddy bear. I was impressed the first time I saw the bear.

When the Holy Spirit told me to "get the bear," I had a vision of the teddy bear. It had a blowup air bladder inside a zippered, brown bear suit. The Holy Spirit impressed me to unzip the bear suit, let the air out of the bladder, and put the air bladder aside. I was left holding a flimsy brown bear suit. I was instructed to drop the empty bear suit on the floor. When I dropped it on the floor, it fell like a silk blouse, without any form. I heard the Holy Spirit say, "That is how people are without Jesus. They have no form or substance."

Then, I was impressed to pick up the bear suit and step inside, so in the vision, I stepped inside the bear suit and pulled up the zipper. As I stood inside the bear suit, the Holy Spirit asked, "What would someone see as they walked past the bear?" I thought, *That is easy; they would see a bear suit.* At that moment, I realized that if I were in Christ Jesus, anyone, Satan included, walking past would see Jesus. Then, I heard the Holy Spirit say, "That is correct. Satan thinks it is Jesus until the person begins to speak with doubt and unbelief." Speaking with doubt and unbelief tells Satan that Jesus is not speaking. I became aware that we must be careful to watch what we say because what we *say always determines the outcome.*

Also, when we are in Christ, others can see Jesus in and through us. One time, I was in a church in Florida. As the pastor shared his message, he never included or referred to God, Jesus, or the Holy Spirit. So I began to pray quietly in tongues—my spiritual language. Soon the message was over, and he invited everyone to stand in the center aisle to receive communion. I continued to pray as those around me discussed who was wearing a new dress or where they were going for lunch. As I stood there, I saw a woman coming toward me from the back of the church. I did not know her; I only knew the two people with me.

When she reached me, she said, "Who are you? I had to come over to meet you because you are so bright." I did not know what she was talking about until later when I learned that the Holy Spirit, the glory of God, resides in us. His glory and brightness can be seen in the darkness. We become a light in the darkness.

Colossians 1:26–27 (NIV), "The mystery that has been kept hidden for ages and generations but is now disclosed to the Lord's people. To them God has chosen to make known among the Gentiles the glorious riches of this mystery, which is Christ in you, the hope of glory."

Our assignments from God show Jesus in us to others. Our attitudes and actions also proclaim Jesus in us. When ministering in India, a friend who was a children's minister used to say, "As Christians, others watch us because they want to know Jesus." I want others to see Jesus in me. How about you?

Another time in India, the Bible school teachers planned to attend a Sunday afternoon service at a local Methodist university. We arrived to find no one there because the students had gone to hear a visiting Evangelist. It was too late for us to join them, so one of our team members suggested we sit in the Father's presence and worship Him. So we sang a couple of worship songs and sat quietly in His presence. We had a wonderful, refreshing time in His presence—not talking or praying—just being with Jesus! When you are in Christ, you have that same privilege to sit in the presence of God anytime you desire. You are part of the family of God. He looks for ways to bless you.

His grace and mercy are new every morning. People see Him shining in and through you, and they want what you have. So take a few minutes to sit and enjoy His presence.

CHAPTER 16:

WHAT IS MY PURPOSE?

The Webster's Dictionary for Students 5th ed. defines *purpose* as "something set up as a goal to be achieved, an aim or intention." We could say a *purpose* is "the aim or goal of a person, what a person is trying to do, or the reason something is used." Your natural purpose is what goals you have or choose to accomplish. Your spiritual purpose is to grow more like Jesus and follow His examples. In this chapter, we will look at your spiritual purpose. You might ask, "How do I do that?"

Ephesians 5:1–2 (NLT), "Imitate God, therefore, in everything you do because you are his dear children. Live a life filled with love, following the example of Christ. He loved us and offered himself as a sacrifice for us, a pleasing aroma to God."

John 15:12 (NKJV), "This is My commandment, that you love one another as I have loved you."

A few years ago, while preparing to teach about our

purpose, the words "as I have loved you" came alive. I thought, *If I am commanded to love others as Jesus loved me, just how did Jesus love me?* I spent some days considering this question and found the answer is multifaceted.

The first part of the answer considers what Jesus did for us. He voluntarily came to earth as a human baby boy. He grew up in a sinful world, but He was without sin, unlike us. At the Father's appointed time, Jesus taught the world how to live a life of love, mercy, and compassion rather than live by the unattainable rules, revenge, and hate. Then, He paid the price for our sin, resulting in the humiliation of death on a cross as a vile criminal, restoring us to the family of God. His death not only paid the price for our sin but removed the control Satan had over us because of that sin. He revealed the Father's love, mercy, and grace for us and made us an heir in the kingdom of God. When Jesus completed the work of redeeming us, He returned to heaven and His place as the Son of God, where He continually intercedes for us. Then, at the appointed time determined only by the Father, (Matthew 24:36; Mark 13:32), Jesus will come again for us so that we may live with God for all eternity in the place He has prepared for us.

Remember there is a God-side and a man-side to everything. Jesus was unique in that He was all God and all man simultaneously. We could not save or deliver ourselves; only Jesus, who was God, could do that. And again, only Jesus, a sinless man, could pay the price of death for our sin. Jesus represented God and man—no one else could do that. Jesus was God who could forgive humanity and also the only man who could pay the price for our sin.

Jesus commands us to love each other as He loved us; we need to walk in love. To do that, we need to define what that means according to the Bible.

> *Jesus replied, "'You must love the Lord your God with all your heart, all your soul, and all your mind.' This is the first and greatest commandment. A second is equally important: 'Love your neighbor as yourself.' The entire law and all the demands of the prophets are based on these two commandments."*
>
> **Matthew 22:37–40 (NLT)**

In this verse, Jesus tells us first to love God with all our heart. Then, He commands us to love others—our neighbors—the same as we love ourselves. This command means we must put aside anger and hate towards others and love them as Jesus loved us. Once we accept who God made us, it is easier to love ourselves and others.

Jesus said the law, and the prophets commanded that we love others. If we love as Jesus commands, we will fulfill all of the commandments. When we love God and others, we cannot be found guilty of violating the law. In the Old Testament, if the children of Israel did not obey the Ten Commandments, they would be separated from the community, and in some cases, they died physically. Jesus brought grace and mercy into our relationship with God.

Next, we need to understand the New Testament definition of love.

> *Love is patient, love is kind. It does not envy, it does not boast, it is not proud. It does not dishonor others, it is not self-seeking, it is not easily angered, it keeps no record of wrongs. Love does not delight in evil but rejoices with the truth. It always protects, always trusts, always hopes, always perseveres. Love never fails.*

1 Corinthians 13:4–8 (NIV)

Now, let us look at the meaning of some specific words in this scripture. Although I am not sure you will find these definitions in any dictionaries, as you study the Word of God, you will see that these words are very complex and have practical meanings for living.

Being *patient* means "remaining calm and not becoming annoyed when waiting for a long time or dealing with problems or difficult people—also being steadfast without complaint despite opposition, difficulty, or adversity."

Being *kind* means "having or showing a gentle nature and desire to help others by doing good things that bring happiness and pleasure to others."

Boasting means "puffing yourself up in speech with excessive pride in who you are, what you possess, or who you know." It is an attempt to show that what you have is better than what others have.

Being *proud* means "having an attitude, presenting

224

yourself as better than others." For example, to suggest you are more important or superior to others.

Being *rude* means "being impolite and not having or showing concern or respect for the rights and feelings of others."

Self-seeking means "only seeking to further your interests while not caring what happens to others."

When you are *easily angered*, you have strong feelings from being upset or annoyed because of something wrong or perceived to be wronged—a strong sense of displeasure that makes someone shout with rage and want to hurt others.

Record of wrongs means "you hang on to and remember all the wrongs of the past. The past is remembered as if it happened today."

Truth is when you rejoice in the truth, not falsehood. You look for what is good, right, and of virtue, not the suffering and misfortune of others.

To *protect* means "to cover or shield from exposure, injury, damage, or destruction by maintaining status or integrity." It is the instinct to keep someone from harm.

Trust is "the belief that the character of someone or something is reliable, good, honest, and dependable."

Persevere means "doing something or trying to do something even though it is difficult, despite opposition or discouragement."

Love never fails; love always succeeds. Love never

stops; it never has doubts.

When you treat yourself and others with Jesus' definition of love, you fulfill Jesus' commandment to love others. And you have another purpose.

> *You are the light of the world. A city that is set on a hill cannot be hidden. Nor do they light a lamp and put it under a basket, but on a lampstand, and it gives light to all who are in the house. Let your light so shine before men, that they may see your good works and glorify your Father in heaven.*
>
> **Matthew 5:14–16 (NKJV)**

You are to be a light in a dark world. Light in this sense is not like turning on a lightbulb to dispel the darkness in a room. Rather, your light is to reveal the love and knowledge of Jesus Christ through your everyday lives with others. Letting your light shine brings people to the knowledge and understanding of Jesus' love for them. This light brings joy to others and glory to our heavenly Father.

Just before Jesus ascended into heaven to return to His Father, He gave His disciples another assignment: they were to share the good news—the gospel of Jesus Christ—with others.

> *Then the eleven disciples went to Galilee, to the mountain where Jesus had told them to go. When they saw him, they worshiped him; but some doubted. Then Jesus came to them and said, "All authority in heaven and*

*on earth has been given to me. Therefore go
and make disciples of all nations, baptizing
them in the name of the Father and of the Son
and of the Holy Spirit, and teaching them to
obey everything I have commanded you. And
surely I am with you always, to the very end
of the age."*

Matthew 28:16–20 (NIV)

Jesus invited His disciples to go to a certain place, where they waited for Him. When Jesus arrived, He told them that Father God had given Him all authority in heaven and earth. (There was no need for Jesus to have control under the earth because He had already taken Satan's power away.) So He gave them all the authority they needed to accomplish the task when He told them to go. Then, He told them He would always be with them. Let's look at Mark's comments on this event.

*And He said to them, "Go into all the world
and preach the gospel to every creature. He
who believes and is baptized will be saved; but
he who does not believe will be condemned.
And these signs will follow those who believe:
In My name they will cast out demons; they
will speak with new tongues; they will take up
serpents; and if they drink anything deadly,
it will by no means hurt them; they will lay
hands on the sick, and they will recover."*

Mark 16:15–18 (NKJV)

Mark commented on the same event as Matthew, but he added some more information. He told them when they preach the gospel signs will follow. These signs would help people believe.

When you are born again and have Jesus living in you, your purpose is to love God, yourself, and others. You become His representative in the world when you tell them about Jesus. People can see Jesus in and through you. When they ask why you seem different, you can tell them what Jesus has done for you. It isn't something weird. Rather, it is the love of God in and through you. You can share your personal experience about how God changed your life and that He can change anyone's life through the love of Jesus in them. But there is more; look at Ephesians chapter 2, verse 10.

Ephesians 2:10 (NLT), "For we are God's masterpiece. He has created us anew in Christ Jesus, so we can do the good things he planned for us long ago."

Finally, this is who you are! You are God's forgiven child, a member of His family, part of the body of Christ. You have been purposely and specially made for His pleasure. You are His masterpiece, his very own piece of valuable art. He loves you, and He calls you His beloved. No one is exactly like you or is as special as you are in His eyes. He brought you here for a time such as this for a special purpose. He will never leave you. The Holy Spirit will teach and show you what to do and tell you what to say in every circumstance. The Passion Translation of the Bible says this even more beautifully.

Ephesians 2:10 (TPT), "We have become His poetry…"

You are God's poetry—His language of love. That is who you are!

Father, speak to those who read this book, giving them a picture of the beautiful person You have created them to be. Give them understanding and wisdom as they seek more of You. Make the assignments You give them shine with Your glory as You work in and through them to bring light into the darkness. Anoint their words with Your fire and passion as they share Jesus with those You have assigned to them. I ask this in Jesus' precious name. Amen and amen.

CHAPTER 17:

THIS IS WHO I AM!

There is a conclusion to this book. Suppose you complete the study of this book and seek God by continuing to study His Word, then you will know, without a doubt, who God is and His characteristics. You will understand how wonderfully He made you and how He loves you unconditionally. Beyond your wildest dreams, you will know that Almighty God, the Creator of the universe, is on your side. He is not angry with you and has forgiven you. Instead, He wants you to know Him personally, to seek Him in all that you do. Then you will know your purpose in life. Finally, you will be able to answer your original question, "Who am I?" For you are a child of God. A member of the family of God. And you will live eternally in the presence of God.

Galatians 3:28 (NIV), "There is neither Jew nor Gentile, neither slave nor free, nor is there male and female, for you are all one in Christ Jesus."

As you allow God's Holy Spirit to lead and guide you, you will also find peace and joy in your life that surpasses your understanding. You will walk through life with awe when you trust Him. Likewise, as you walk in your new life, the glory of God in you will touch others, bringing them peace and joy too.

Now you can say, "This is who I am!"

> *Now may the God of peace, who through the blood of the eternal covenant brought back from the dead our Lord Jesus, that great Shepherd of the sheep, equip you with everything good for doing his will, and may he work in us what is pleasing to him, through Jesus Christ, to whom be glory for ever and ever. Amen.*

> **Hebrews 13:20–21 (NIV)**

BIBLIOGRAPHY

Bevere, John. *The Bait of Satan*. Lake Mary: Charisma House, 2014.

Davis, Geron. "Mercy Saw Me." Track 11 on *Amen (Live)*. Integrity Music, 2008.

Eberhard, David M., Gary F. Simons, and Charles S. Fleming, eds. *Ethnologue: Languages of the World*. Dallas: SIL International, 2021.

Fortune, Don, and Katie Fortune. *Discover Your God-Given Gifts*. Grand Rapids: Chosen Books div. Baker Book House Company, 1987.

Graham, Billy. Does God Have Hands and Eyes and Feet? Billy Graham Evangelistic Association, 2006.

Got Questions.org. "What does it mean that God is our Abba Father." 2002-2022, Got Questions Ministries, www.GotQuestions.org. Latest access: June 6, 2022.

Hayford, Jack. *New Spirit Filled Life Bible Notes*. Nashville: Thomas Nelson Bibles, 2002.

Josephus. *Josephus. The Complete Works*. Nashville: Thomas Nelson Publishers, 1998.

Schaff, Philip. *The Pocket Bible Dictionary*. Lebanon: Jubilee Publishers, Inc., 1996.

Stallings, Stacy. *The Easy Way Out*. Spirit of Light Publishing, 2013.

Strong, James. *The New Strong's Complete Dictionary of Bible Words.* Nashville: Thomas Nelson Publishers, Inc., 1996.

Zodhiates, Spiros. *The Hebrew-Greek Key Study Bible.* Grand Rapids: Baker Book House, 1984.

ABOUT THE AUTHOR

Ruth Pettengill James was born into a Christian family whose parents taught her to respect and value the things of God—teaching not only in words but by their Christian walk.

In 1972, when Ruth's father was murdered, she blamed God for her father's death and moved away from Him. Then in 1975, Ruth suffered a painful divorce. Unable to deal with the grief and losses, she attempted suicide in 1976; Ruth went into heaven and stood before the Lord Jesus. He told her, "I have work for you to do, so you cannot stay; you must go back. Always remember I love you." After "running" from God for several more years, in 1980, Ruth recommitted her life to Jesus. In 1982, God defined the work He had called her to do: "Teach My children" was the assignment.

After graduating from Rhema Bible Training Center in Broken Arrow, Oklahoma, in May 1991, Ruth began Amana International Ministries to teach God's children. In addition, Ruth taught and ministered as a missionary to India, Hong Kong, the Philippines, China, Russia, the Dominican Republic, Jamacia, and the United States, teaching in Bible schools, special meetings, and churches.

Since 2018, Ruth has been teaching an in-depth study of the Old Testament and how it points to Jesus and to the end of time as we know it.

Through technology, Ruth continues to teach God's children, both in her community and the world. Recently, Ruth stepped into God's call to publish several books, beginning with Who Am I?, which teaches people who God is, who they are, and how much He loves them.

SCRIPTURE INDEX

Genesis 1:1 32

Genesis 1:1–2 60

Genesis 1:26–27. .113, 147

Genesis 1:31 113

Genesis 2:7 . . . . 41, 113, 136

Genesis 2:15–17. . . . . .41, 148

Genesis 2:18 . . . . .42, 148

Genesis 2:20–23. 150

Genesis 2:21–23. 42

Genesis 3:1–7 151

Genesis 3:6 152

Genesis 3:7 153

Genesis 3:8–10. 36

Genesis 3:21 154

Genesis 3:22 154

Genesis 10:32 199

Genesis 11:1. 199

Genesis 12:1–4. 27

Genesis 17:3–6. 27

Genesis 49:10 128

Exodus 3:2. 197

Exodus 3:14–15 25

Exodus 12:37–38, 40–41 26

Exodus 24:17 198

Exodus 33:17–20 85

Leviticus 11:44 208

Leviticus 17:11, 14 114

Leviticus 19:1–2 87

Numbers 23:19 74

Deuteronomy 7:9 89

Deuteronomy 31:8 51

1 Samuel 16:5–7 127

Psalm 8:3–8 116

Psalm 8:4–6 1

Psalm 17:8 21

Psalm 24:1 . . . . .32, 148

Psalm 25:8–10 85

Psalm 27:13 86

Psalm 32:8–9 144

Psalm 68:20 159

Psalm 84:11 101

Psalm 86:5 102

Psalm 91:1–2 65

Psalm 91:14–16 76

Psalm 95:7 54

Psalm 103:12 103

Psalm 105:8–10 28

Psalm 106:1 98

Psalm 111:10 122

Psalm 119:105 136

Psalm 130:4 103

Psalm 139:7–12 83

Psalm 139:13–16 120

Psalm 139:13–18 11

Psalm 139:16 144

Psalm 145:8 98

Proverbs 1:7 122

Proverbs 6:16–19 75

Proverbs 9:10 122

Proverbs 20:27 137

Proverbs 31:25–30 3

Isaiah 43:18 81

Isaiah 43:25 104

Isaiah 53:5–6 170

Isaiah 53:10 170

Isaiah 55:10–11 95

Isaiah 55:11 90

Isaiah 59:16 159

Jeremiah 29:11–13 . . . . .144, 210

Jeremiah 31:3. 76

Jeremiah 32:38–41. 29

Joel 2:28–29. 192

Amos 3:7 16

Micah 7:18. 104

Micah 7:18–19. 98

Haggai 2:8 157

Zechariah 4:6. 213

Malachi 3:6 90

Matthew 1:1. 28

Matthew 1:18–25. 160

Matthew 1:21. 174

Matthew 3:13–17. 181

Matthew 4:23. 57

Matthew 5:14–16. 226

Matthew 7:7–8. 215

Matthew 7:7–11 87

Matthew 10:26. 17

Matthew 17:20. 92

Matthew 22:37–40 223

Matthew 28:16–20 227

Matthew 28:18–20 182

Mark 1:4–5 180

Mark 4:22–23. 17

Mark 11:22–25. 93

Mark 11:23–26. 214

Mark 11:25. 104

Mark 14:36 38

Mark 16:15–18. 227

Mark 16:17 203

Luke 1:26–35. 48

Luke 2:1–5. 162

Luke 3:23. 48

Luke 4:40. 57

Luke 6:38. 155

Luke 23:39–43. 185

Luke 24:7. 49

John 1:1–4 163

John 1:1–5 46

John 1:1–5, 14 33

John 1:14 . . . . .46, 163

John 1:14, 17 46

John 1:29–34 181

John 1:43–45 190

John 3:16 . . . . .45, 175

John 3:16–17 . . . . .45, 77, 164

John 3:36 56

John 4:10 . . . . .52, 168

John 4:13-14 168

John 4:24 . . . . .23, 73

John 4:39–42 169

John 5:24 56

John 6:35 52

John 6:40 173

John 6:47 169

John 7:38 168

John 8:12 53

John 8:31–32 53

John 8:44 152

John 10:7 54

John 10:10 . . . . .56, 80, 159

John 10:14–15 54

John 10:30 52

John 11:25–26 56

John 13:34 . . . . .83, 173

John 14:1 132

John 14:1–7 50

John 14:6 57

John 14:6–7 52

John 14:9 52

John 14:10–11 206

John 14:15–17 61

John 14:20 207

John 14:26 62

John 15:4–8 68

John 15:7 213

John 15:9–13 69

John 15:12 . . . . .105, 221

John 15:26 62

John 16:7–11 63

John 16:7–15 60

John 16:13 62

John 16:23–24 215

John 20:22 172

Acts 1:8 . . . . .189, 194

Acts 1:9 50

Acts 2:1–6 194

Acts 2:3–4 196

Acts 2:5–8 199

Acts 8:5–8, 12 191

Acts 8:14–17 191

Acts 10:44–46 200

Acts 19:1–6 193

Romans 2:29 187

Romans 3:23–24 101

Romans 3:23–25 41

Romans 5:1 132

Romans 5:1–2 100

Romans 5:8–9 43

Romans 5:18–21 173

Romans 6:3–4 184

Romans 6:23 . . . . 40, 49, 153, 171

Romans 8:1–2 211

Romans 8:16–17 164

Romans 8:28 37

Romans 8:35, 37–39 .39

Romans 8:37–39 79

Romans 10:9–10 182

Romans 10:9–13 176

Romans 10:17 92

Romans 11:36 32

Romans 12:3 92

Romans 12:6–8 140

1 Corinthians 1:7–9 .89

1 Corinthians 2:1–8 .18

1 Corinthians 2:9–12 18

1 Corinthians 2:11 137

1 Corinthians 2:16 124

1 Corinthians 3:16 . . . . .64, 138

1 Corinthians 12:4–11 140

1 Corinthians 13:4–8 224

1 Corinthians 13:8 79

1 Corinthians 14:2–3 201

1 Corinthians 14:4 201

1 Corinthians 14:10 200

1 Corinthians 14:14–15 201

1 Corinthians 14:22–25 202

1 Corinthians 14:27 202

1 Corinthians 15:50–53 80

2 Corinthians 3:17 73

2 Corinthians 3:18 207

2 Corinthians 4:16 207

2 Corinthians 5:17 206

2 Corinthians 5:21 .49, 170, 206

2 Corinthians 6:18 37

2 Corinthians 12:9 102

Galatians 2:20 183

Galatians 3:16 29

Galatians 3:26–28 205

Galatians 3:26–29 . . . . .165, 187

Galatians 3:28 . . . . .11, 231

Galatians 3:29 30

Galatians 4:4–7 . . . . .46, 165

Galatians 5:22–23 67

Galatians 5:26 106

Ephesians 1:7. 100

Ephesians 1:7–8 164

Ephesians 2:4–5 98

Ephesians 2:4–6 216

Ephesians 2:4–9 183

Ephesians 2:10 . . . . 119, 209, 228, 229

Ephesians 3:20 145

Ephesians 4:1–7 184

Ephesians 4:4–6 34

Ephesians 4:11–13 139

Ephesians 4:32 107

Ephesians 5:1–2 221

Philippians 1:6 145

Philippians 2:3–4 106

Philippians 2:13 145

Philippians 3:12–14 82

Philippians 4:6–7 . . . . 96, 131, 213

Colossians 1:13–14 171

Colossians 1:26–27 .205, 218

Colossians 2:13–15 .171, 212

Colossians 3:13 106

1 Thessalonians 5:23 120

1 Thessalonians 5:23–24 .145

2 Timothy 1:9. 100

2 Timothy 3:16–17. 16

Titus 1:1–2. 75

Hebrews 1:14. 118

Hebrews 3:1–6. 55

Hebrews 4:12. 121

Hebrews 4:12–13. 136

Hebrews 4:14–16. 56

Hebrews 4:16. .51, 102

Hebrews 9:7. 138

Hebrews 10:16–17. 29

Hebrews 10:17. 104

Hebrews 10:23. 89

Hebrews 11:1. 91

Hebrews 11:6. .91, 134

Hebrews 12:29. 198

Hebrews 13:8. 90

Hebrews 13:20–21. .232

James 1:5–8. . . . . .93, 134, 214

James 1:12–17. 86

James 2:23. 28

James 4:7. . . . . .80, 111

James 4:7–8. . . . . .80, 212

James 4:7–8, 10. 153

James 5:13–16 135

1 Peter 1:14–16 88

1 Peter 2:9 138

1 Peter 3:3–4 126

1 Peter 5:7 . . . . .51, 132

1 John 1:9 . . . . .89, 103

1 John 2:1 63

1 John 3:1 . . . . .38, 106

1 John 4:8 . . . . .37, 48

1 John 4:9–10 76

1 John 4:19 37

1 John 5:7–8 33

Jude 1:20-21 201

Revelation 1:4 25

Revelation 12:9 151